On the Rails

A Journey around America by train

First Edition 2010 Lulu.Com
ISBN 978-1-4475-0663-8

Jamie Sutherland

Chapters

Acknowledgements

Many thanks go to all of those who helped me out, put me up or put up with me. Special thanks to the Family Payne: Gill, Stuart, Georgia and Matthew. Thanks also to Tom Church who was actually able to find a useful application for his degree by editing this book. Thanks to Amber and Greg in Seattle for putting up with a tourist and finally Liz, who kept the drink flowing.

"Everybody might just be one big soul. Well it looks that-a-way to me..."

-Woody Guthrie

For Ash

Who is coming with me next time

Part I:

Life, Liberty and the Pursuit of Emptiness

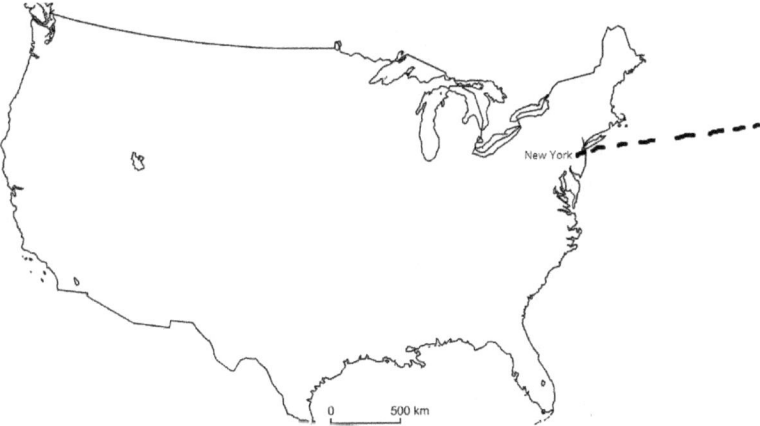

Sometime between the stupefying boredom of a 3am Wednesday night shift and the barely organized chaos of a Friday night stretch, I realize that I have to get away. It's June, and I'm working for a part of the public sector that prefers its employees not to talk about it too much. The mad crush to obtain some peak time off has left us short staffed and overworked, on-top of which I'm trying to cram for a career-in-the-balance professional exam, due in early September. Come September though, and everyone will have returned, work will have slackened, my exam will be over, and the familiar rhythm will have returned. An ideal time then to get the hell out of Dodge, and push off for a month long adventure. Now, even within the public sector, this takes some planning and a modicum of sycophantic brown nosing. But, after some gentle negotiation, my boss's, boss's, boss has signed off, and I have an entire month to fill.

During quiet night shift, a plan takes form. I've travelled to America before, but the sheer size of the country denies the feeling that you have really 'done' it, mostly because you haven't. Flying between cities feels like making tiny pin-pricks in the huge landmass, and driving; though true to a romanticized, on-the-road ideal, would take many months, if not years. The previous summer, two friends and I hired a car and took off; driving from Vegas through Nevada, Arizona, Utah and Colorado. It took a week and still, at the end, the overwhelming impression was just how much we hadn't seen, rather than how much we had. Staring at a Google map of the country, I find my inspiration; a train adventure. I will circumnavigate the entire US border, from North to South, East to West and back again. I will 'do' America, in a strictly geographical and topographical sense.

From New York I will head down the East coast to Miami, leaving West to stop off in Houston, before continuing West all the way to LA and the Pacific Ocean. From there, I'll go North to San Francisco, then all the way North to Seattle. Finally, back east, from Seattle to Chicago, and then back to New York. I will do two trans-continent crossings, spend approximately 120 hours on trains, and pack in as much fun stuff as I can en-route including indulging my favourite pastimes of Jiu-jitsu, running and moderately heavy drinking.

America is blessed with a single rail company, Amtrak, which is something of a sideshow oddity in a country where the aircraft is king. Part of the reason for this is that Amtrak is slow, very slow. Passenger trains play second fiddle to the massive freight trains that ride the same rails. Even when the lines are free, the trains rarely top a modest 70mph - faster than driving, but nothing compared to the high speed rail networks of Europe or Japan. Still, for a fraction under four hundred pounds, Amtrak will sell you a one month rail pass (coach class) which affords the holder a reserved seat and unlimited travel around America. At this point, the longest I have spent on a train was eight hours - from the South to Aberdeen. My overriding memory of this journey was that it was hellish. Stumbling out of Aberdeen Station after attempting to sleep in a chair I was accosted by a persistent prostitute who offered me tea, two slices of toast and a blow-job at a package deal price (enterprising, but no thank-you). The journey from Seattle to Chicago will last forty eight hours. I hope they do toast.

In order to maximize my holiday time; I work a full night shift the day before I go away, pushing through till six in the morning. Adrenaline, a cheap non-branded red-bull substitute and the fact that I haven't packed yet, helps to keep me awake. On the way home from a mercifully easy night, I stop at the supermarket to pick up a breakfast of chilled champagne, pan-au-chocolate and flowers for my girlfriend Ash, who has raised very little objection to my heading off for a month alone. My Mother didn't raise no fool, as I'm sure they say somewhere.

Several glasses of champers later and I grab a couple of hours sleep before packing my rucksack, my day sack and my magically folding bike (purchased especially for this trip) and we head to Heathrow. It will later become apparent that this rather hasty packing procedure will account for why I remember to bring jiu-jitsu gear, wrestling gear, running gear, wetsuit, but only two t-shirts and three socks, none of which match.

After getting safely checked in at Heathrow, Ash and I hit the pub for a final pint. She is almost as excited for my trip as I am and I feel bad that she's not coming with me. We drink up and I make my way to the gatee and a flight with the entirely anonymous airline Delta. Or was it United? In any case, I land in NYC late Saturday night. An uneventful flight leads to a pleasingly hassle free entry at the border. Mercifully, the ritual of filling out the green landing-card is gone, so you no longer have to answer such soul searching questions as: "Are you a Nazi war criminal on the run?" and "Is it your intent to overthrow the Government?" (It is a fair bet that answering yes to these questions would lead to an interesting conversation at the border, and a rapid change of holiday plans). I'm out of the plane, through immigration and into a yellow cab inside of thirty minutes. Traffic is light, and as the driver picks up speed to the Lincoln Tunnel, I open the window and let the warm and muggy New York air fill the cab. A great sense of relief comes over me. My train South doesn't leave for three days; I have time to see the city. I get to the hostel in up-town Manhattan, exhausted and with the intention of crashing, but my new dorm roomies; three English girls and singularly unpleasant South African chap, would like to get beers. Oh well, be rude not to, sometimes it's best not to stop and catch your breath. Several beers in a tavern off Broadway later, and I can breathe out; I'm in NYC, with a roll of fifties in my side pocket, train ticket in the back, and a whole month in front of me. Bliss.

Sunday morning and I rise early, body clock not entirely in synch with local time. I leave my snoring roomies and quietly slip out with my newly purchased folding mountain bike, which is garnering envious looks from early bird travellers in the lobby. On the corner of 112th and Broadway is the famous, yet pleasingly down-at-heel, 'Tom's Restaurant' that was featured in American snore-fest 'Seinfeld' and immortalized in a Suzanne Vega song that wasn't very good. I get pancakes. After a relaxed breakfast and the New York Sunday Times (makes our Sunday Times look like the abridged version) I ride down town to the New York Buddhist Centre, where, following the previous day's anniversary of the 9/11 attacks, they are saying prayers for world peace and meditating a bit. The avenues are traffic free at this time and as I zip down them on my bike I wonder why more New Yorkers don't travel this way. I will find this out in about 24 hours' time, but for now, I have the carefree smug feeling that cycling in the sun brings.

After some meditation and a talk on the theme of emptiness, it's over to Washington Square for lunch. It transpires that Washington Square is holding a dog festival called 'Dogpoloza', or something. The whole exercise is an attempt to raise money for dog charities and to hold the dog equivalent of a date auction, where formerly stray dogs are introduced on stage and the assembled crowd is encouraged to adopt them. I watch as an extraordinarily enthusiastic female compare, who would be a shoe-in for a spot on 'The Apprentice', introduces us to 'Freddie'. Freddie is a 98 pound Bull Mastiff cross. It's not revealed what the cross bit is, but from the look of him I'm guessing that its wildebeest. Anyway, the woman explains that "Freddie was found wandering lost in Central Park, looking for somebody to love him and give him a 'forever home'." Freddie looks on with malevolent disinterest. I suspect that actually young Freddie was wandering Central Park looking for somebody to eat, before sleeping any damn place he pleased.

Back up-town and it's time for my first session of Bikram Yoga. For those of you who don't know, Bikram is 90 minutes of hardcore yogic hell. The room is heated to near sauna temperatures and the poses are designed to raise your heart rate to an unacceptable level. It is also performed damn near naked, due to the heat and the fact that most of the adherents are essentially posers. I can't wait. Next to me in class is 'Alex'. Alex is a pasty looking young fellow who seems nervous. He should be: ten minutes into the session Alex collapses, rises for a second, and then throws up. And I don't mean a little bit of puke, I mean a full on 10-pint-and-a-kebab-hurl. So not only is it sweltering hot, but the whole studio now smells of Alex's sick. Christ. At the end of the session we all applaud Alex for getting through his first session, and presumably, for not ralphing a second time.

Clearing the smell of Alex's epic fail from my nostrils, I take an afternoon stroll around some old haunts. I first came to New York by myself in the Summer of 2004. At the time, I was short on both money and common sense so decided to stay at the cheapest hostel in the city, in lower Harlem. Heading back there, I come to Frederick Douglass circle, essentially a large roundabout. It has taken the local authority years to do it, but the circle has now been restored, with stone benches surrounding an imposing statute of Douglass himself. Frederick Douglass was an escaped slave who took the Underground Railroad North of the Mason Dixon Line, to freedom. Once there, he wrote what has to be the most succinct account of the ridiculousness of one human being having dominion over another. This work; 'Narrative of a Life', isn't just an angry account of one man's slavery, but a disbelievingly furious expression of just how such a preposterous system could have been allowed in the first place. Educated, charismatic and forthright, Douglass became one of the most outspoken opponents of the slavery in the South, and the inherent racism and sexism of the North.

Douglass is therefore an important figure in Black American history, and like many such figures (King, X, Garvey) is honoured with a Harlem landmark. Frederick Douglass Circle used to demark the end of the Upper West Side, and the start of Harlem. Crossing the Circle, going North of 110th street, one could notice an immediate and distinct change in character and atmosphere. Just yards from some of the most expensive real estate on earth, extreme poverty was out in the open, alongside drug dealing, social deprivation and gang related violence, yet set against a vibrant, proud and culturally important community. No longer. Like a rising tide, the area has become slowly gentrified, and Harlem is in full retreat in the face of rising property prices, redevelopment and new business. Not all of the changes have been bad. When I first visited, and stayed for a month, the constant begging and hustling became wearing. So did being offered crack when you were looking for nothing more potent than a courgette. Also gone are the homeless who used to sleep on filthy mattresses on the corner of 113th, just by the hostel. Yet not for one minute do I believe that they all simultaneously got over the various health, drug and social problems that put them there and wandered off to become productive members of society. But wherever they went they took the community atmosphere with them. Gone are the street BBQ's, the all night card and domino games played on the steps of houses in the balmy August night-time heat, and in their place, smoothie bars, exclusive restaurants, and unaffordable studio flats. The basketball court has now been replaced with a nicely laid soccer pitch. Yes, Harlem is in retreat, and nobody knows how far back it has to go. Still, on the plus side, it's much easier to buy a courgette there these days.

A stone's throw away on Broadway, the area is buzzing on what is still a hot and sunny Sunday afternoon. The new semester has just started, and the area is chock full of new and returning Columbia University students- some of the brightest, and most privileged young people in the country. Signs on shops welcome them back, the cafés are full and on the sidewalks, the book hawks have a great trade going. The book hawks are interesting characters. Daily setting up their trestle tables with second hand books, sourced from God knows where. The selections are random, but largely highbrow, and clearly aimed at the more budget conscious student with a long reading list.

Dostoevsky competes with advanced algebra for space while browsers and potential customers root about. The hawks themselves have more important matters to attend to however: Chess. On recovered pieces of chipboard balanced on beer crates, some of the most battered boards and pieces in the history of the game play out matches that are as fast as they are competitive. The standard of chess is high, but sportsmanship is at a premium: the hawks specialize in chess smack talk, designed to throw off and infuriate an opponent into a momentary lapse of concentration (and one suspects, to provide a little bit of a show for the gawking tourists). Genuine chess connoisseurs, and this city has its share, stand around kibitzing with each other in indecipherable mumblings. Games don't end with a handshake here, the loser simply gets up and walks off, quickly replaced by another hawk, and the endless game of speed chess and insults resumes as quickly as it ended. The best bit is that you can play too - for a price. The chess hustlers in Washington Square play for dollar bets on five minute blitz games - then proceed to blast the ill-prepared opponent off the board with astoundingly fast play, smack talk, and, if they can, with sleights of hand that would make a magician proud. The hawks are a little different. The games have to be slower to allow for the necessary distraction of actually serving customers. This means that they need to get paid either way (except when playing each other - when temporary bragging rights, no less valuable, are all that is at stake). This means that a game will cost you a dollar, but it doesn't have to be on the clock. Win or lose, you pay, but that doesn't mean that the hawk won't be trying- crowds gather for the close games, and for really close games the other hawks might come over; pride is very much at stake. I'm in.

It doesn't take long to get a game. My opponent, who has an excellent range of Graham Greene books, looks like a 60's jazz poet. Black cracked skin and a long grey goatee beard are topped off with a black beret and a deep growling voice. I take the white pieces and breathe in. The game moves along apace. It's easy to make a mistake under these conditions so I play an opening line designed to create a long, slow, and boring strategic game, devoid of the tactical explosions that can lead to a very quick implosion. Jazz poet rolls out the distraction tactics to begin with, but we're not playing on clocks here, and when it becomes apparent that it's not working, and the game develops into something a little interesting, it slowly fades as his concentration deepens. A little crowd builds, including another hawk who takes the seat next to Jazz Man, looking over his shoulder and silently nodding behind huge dark glasses. Jazz Man is playing aggressively now, building up a huge, if obvious attack on the open g-file. He's miscalculated though, his attack is going nowhere, and I've got a passed pawn, zipping down the board, promotion bound. Too late, Jazz Man realises what is going on, and is forced into a costly piece exchange to prevent it. All is not lost yet, but now the pressure is on - the other hawk is smiling broadly, and I suspect that Jazz Man is at serious risk of a roasting if he loses to the obvious tourist who couldn't be much squarer in this crowd. He moves, he blunders, but doesn't see it until I sweep his rook from the board. It's not check mate yet, but it is game over, and he knows it. True to form, Jazz Man doesn't resign, he just gets up to leave. I'm not having it. Chess has its own etiquette that is observed from the frozen Siberian wastes to the Reform Club in London - and they're the ones in breach of it. I stand and extend my hand across the board. Jazz Man hesitates, mumbles something and looks away but begrudgingly extends two fingers, bound with a rubber band that I promptly shake. I pick up my rucksack and move on, suppressing a goofy grin until I'm round the corner, adrenaline mixing with the morning's caffeine to create a dizzying buzz.

Back at the hostel I have new roomies, and they want to go for beers. This has got to be the single best thing about hostelling - the never ending stream of instant friends that are available, if you are open to it and you don't look like a maniac. Of course, it's also a very cheap way to travel, but I'm always surprised by the number of people who I meet travelling, who could easily afford the luxury of a private room and a toilet that will absolutely definitely work, but instead opt for the more acquired pleasures of sharing a room with up to twelve strangers, in bunk beds. The only comparable living conditions are prison, which I suppose you have less choice in. Still, things are nowhere near as grim as my more well-heeled friends would like to imagine. The near real-time feedback that is provided by guests on the omnipresent booking website -'hostel world.com' has served to relentlessly drive standards up. Hostels are on an improvement curve that bends towards funkiness - and the axis appear to be labeled 'wi-fi' availability and 'fun'. Like most people, when checking out hostels, I mostly look at the photos, then the price, then the overall rating (an aggregate score of visitor reviews) and then read the last half dozen or so reviews to get low-down on what people who stayed there in the last week thought of the place, so if they have recently employed a miserable unhelpful git on the front desk-you'll know about it, and can avoid them. Book the hostel through hostelworld.com and you can add your own review minutes after checking out, sometimes while still using their wi-fi. Of course the hostel gets the right of reply: I recall one memorable review of a hostel where a recent guest called 'James', had left a withering review, complaining about just about everything, before giving the hostel a savage twenty percent overall score. The hostel owner left a reply to his review that simply read: "I remember James - he was an asshole". But anyway, now there is free-wi-fi in every hostel in North America, and for all I know, the world. I've stayed in four star hotels that tried to charge me ten pounds a night for the same. And those hotels just aren't fun. Sure; you don't have to buy a secure padlock to keep your underwear safe, and you almost never get woken up during the night by the sound of a bunk-mate masturbating, but I've always found them relentless, soulless and depressing, especially when travelling alone. I'll stick with hostels. Out with my roomies I last for just about two pints before the last 48 hours catch up with me and I duck out early, back to my bunk bed and sleep heavily. The next morning the unpleasant South African chap complains loudly about someone "cracking the bag-pipes last night". I'm saying nothing. Mostly because I'm not 100% sure what it means.

Monday. Today is exercise day. Full of enthusiasm I'm out early for a pleasant run in Central Park before catching a mid-morning Bikram session. Then it's back into the park for a picnic of Swiss-cheese and gherkin sandwiches and a long nap under a tree. It's sunny and everybody seems to be in a good mood. Two hours later, things have changed; a storm is brewing and judging by the dark clouds on the horizon, it's going to be a dousie. Undeterred I hop on my bike and start down-town where I am due for a two hour Brazilian Jiu-jitsu session with three-time world champion Vitor 'Shaolin' Ribero.

Brazilian jiu-jitsu is a far distant cousin of its Japanese ancestor. An offshoot of Judo, mixed with wrestling and forged in the violent streets and favelas of Brazil in the early 20th century, it is a very up close and personal martial art and practiced, overwhelmingly, by men. Or, as one of my friends once commented: "It's a bit homoerotic, isn't it?" Extreme physical proximity with sweaty men notwithstanding, there's gold in them there hills: In the early 90's the Brazilian masters, principally from the legendary Gracie family, realized that rich Americans would pay top-dollar for a martial art that actually worked and didn't involve learning dance steps or mastering a death touch. So began a great migration of Brazilian black belts that continues to this day.

Anyway, nicknames are big in BJJ and I'm training with one 'Shaolin'. My nickname is the slightly less fearsome 'Cake', earned not in the blood-soaked-no-rules fights of Rio's darkest favelas, but in a German café after miss-advisedly ordering two portions of desert in front of my teammates. Oh well. By the time I'm on the road, the heavens have opened. It's rush hour, and in the semi-darkness taxis weave in and out with little, if any, care for cyclists. The road gets slippery, the drivers get bad tempered and overhead. Set above the sky-scrapers of mid-town, dramatically massive forks of lightening are crashing down. It goes from terrifying to exhilarating and back to just plain terrifying.

By the time I've found the first floor gym I'm soaked to the skin, so I'm pleased to get a warm reception from the nice girl on the front desk. When I arrive Shaolin is giving a heartfelt lecture to the junior class on the evils of drinking. At the far end of the gym a number of senior grades shuffle their feet and look slightly guilty. I slip into the changing rooms and suit up, getting back on the mat just in time for the traditional bowing. Shortly into our warm-up Shaolin himself comes over to introduce himself and chat for a bit - he's no stranger to the UK, having competed in the country's now defunct 'Cage Rage' fight organization. MMA is all well and good, but Shaolin made his name in the BJJ world championships, and his teaching is high on technical details, and general bonhomie. Our class includes an hour of hard sparring. I do pleasingly well and don't embarrass myself- although it doesn't come easy. Shaolin is picking the sparring partners and points me towards a hulking mass of a man, a brown belt no less, who is kneeling patiently on one side of the dojo. Lined up against him, waiting for the direction to start, I can't help but notice his ears - heavy, heavy cauliflowering going on here. Cauliflower ears are the unmistakable mark of a man who has spent many hours of hard time on the mat, and are worn with pride by the owner, although many jiu-jitsu players who are more mindful of how they are going to look in the mirror (or who have girlfriends) go to some lengths to avoid them. Such is the machismo of the sport that a senior grade without at least mildly deformed ears may well be looked down on, to such an extent that there are stories of Brazilian fighters vigorously rubbing their ears with the rough gi's to speed up the whole process. My girlfriend Ash is having none of it however, and regularly checks my ears after training sessions. No gi-rubbing for me then. Still my opponent is a friendly chap, and although he gives me a fairly good drubbing he later pays me the very jiu-jitsu compliment of "strong neck" after failing to strangle me unconscious with a collar choke that could be modestly described as 'uncomfortable'.

At the end of the session I take a souvenir photo with Shaolin and tell him about my plans, although I do resist the temptation to buy a t-shirt emblazoned with the words: "Vitor Shaolin is my Homeboy" (was a close run thing though) and then it's out the door and back onto a now dark and rainy street in downtown Manhattan.

Back at the hostel and yet more roomies, who, unsurprisingly want to.... go for beers. Enough. I'm out of here in the morning, starting my trek around America. Instead I decide to stay in and take a trip up to the hostel's rooftop patio. Several floors up and overlooking Harlem, a small party is developing as the assembled guests flout the hostel's 'no alcohol' policy while a couple of back-packers strum acoustic guitars. The late-summer night air is muggy, but leaning over the balcony I can take in the city and people watch the streets below. Several years ago, standing in the same spot and surrounded by a similar crowd, I witnessed one of the most shocking incidents I've seen; in New York or anywhere else: a very large man, with a great big blinging chain was walking down the street with a woman on either arm. They were in high spirits, laughing and shouting when they came across a group of homeless people on the street corner, directly below the hostel. The homeless were bedded down under cardboard. The troupe stopped and started to laugh, shout and point "oh GOD, look they're NAKED under there!" In short order, the shouting turned to violence as bling man started to quite literally put the boot in- viciously kicking the prone sleepers. The scene was partially obscured by the corner of the hostel, but the shouting and joyful encouragement of the two banshee-like women left no doubt as to what was going on. The noise broke up the patio party and everyone was now leaning over the balcony rail to see what was happening. And what was happening didn't stop - bling man carried on kicking and insulting his victims. The whole thing was sickening, so much so that it took me a time to realize that a number of the young hostellers were staring over at me, as if waiting for me to do something. But do what? I didn't have a mobile phone, there were no members of staff about, and looking around the very young backpacking crowd who suddenly all resembled school children, the chance of recruiting a posse looked distant at best. So I hesitated and did nothing, but bling-man wasn't stopping and I realized that this was probably going to be one of those moments that you look back on and question just why you didn't intervene. So with a sick feeling in my stomach and no small amount of total fucking fear, I ran off the patio, down three flights of stairs and out of the hostel. Turning the corner to the street I slowed down to a quick-step: as a man who knew about such things once told me: "run to a fire, walk to a fight". Catching my breath as I turned the final corner of the hostel I realized that I had no plan whatsoever for what I was about to do, and that this too might be a moment that I looked back on with some regret. Walking slowly next to a chain link fence I could see some people moving, but the noise had stopped- bling man and his ghastly women were gone; leaving several sorry looking homeless people dusting themselves off and re-arranging their possessions. One saw me and stared. I paused, considered saying something, but nothing came to me and with bling man gone there was nothing else to do but slowly back away and return to the hostel, just another unpleasant incident in a city that regularly sees worse. Back on the patio I retook my place - a couple of the backpackers were staring at me, "They're fine", I told them, although that didn't really describe their situation. Truth be known I didn't really want to think about it, I still felt sick, but very grateful to have emerged unscathed. Just another 'what if' scenario.

Reverie over, I look down at the spot where it happened: no homeless there now, just an alley-cat sniffing about in the orange glow of the street light. It's time for bed- I'm heading South for Miami Beach in the morning, where I plan to wrestle a man with the even better nick name of 'Cyborg'...

Optimist Dog, 113th and Broadway

Washington Square

Hanging out in Times Square you meet all sorts of folk

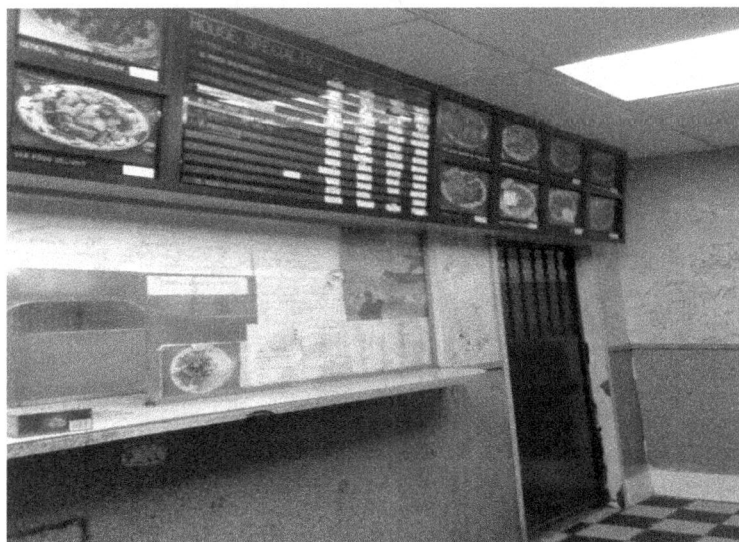

Possibly the worst take out ever, just round the corner from the hostel (note graffiti *inside* of shop)

Mid-town , New York

Jamie "The Cake" Sutherland with Vitor "Shaolin" Ribeiro. He's my homeboy you know.

Part II

Bound for Glory

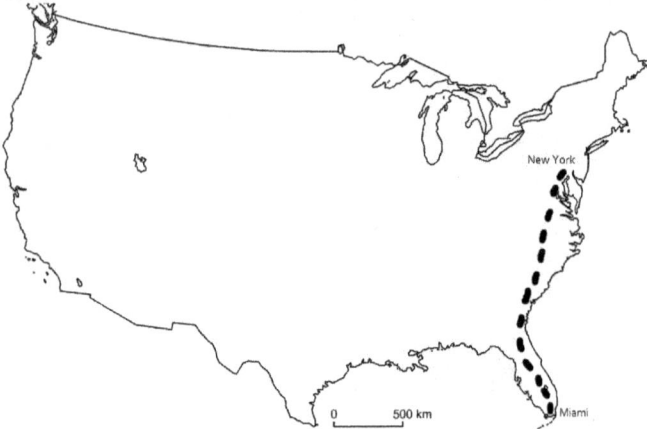

New York City, early Tuesday morning, I walk out of the still quiet hostel to my favourite, and very hip, up-town book store to purchase reading matter for my long journey ahead. I opt for Woody Guthrie's autobiography "Bound for Glory" the story of how Woody travelled the US throughout the years of the great depression, riding the railroads, hiding in box cars and recording some of the earliest known American folk songs. Woody's songs stood in protest about a society that was becoming unbalanced by wage inequality and the terrible social deprivation wrought by the depression. Infused throughout his songs though was a hard-bitten optimism and celebration of the working man, realized most famously in the often covered song: "This Land is Your Land", which would go on to inspire generations of American song writers such as Pete Seger, Bob Dylan and Bruce Springsteen. Remarkably Woody achieved all of this with a singing voice that makes Bob Dylan sound like Aretha Franklin. Towards the end of his career Woody sat down to write the autobiography I've just purchased for five dollars and I'm treating it as something of a guide book, a bit like the Lonely Planet, but more comprehensive. For example; it includes useful advice on signing credit notes with apricot farmers (don't) and on fighting hobo's in box-cars (best not, but sometimes unavoidable). Woody had a travel light philosophy, and I can relate to that a bit, although I've actually purchased a ticket, which somewhat minimises the chances of getting a damn good hiding from a railway 'Bull'. The chance of getting into a fight with a hobo remains omnipresent however.

The weather forecast for Miami is 32 degrees; either my increasingly floppy hair or the holiday beard is going to have to go. Well, it wouldn't be a holiday without a beard. So I pop up town to Harlem where I find a little Dominican barber shop that is open at 8.am. My barber, Eduardo, is very friendly and clearly takes pride in his old school barbering skills. Unfortunately Eduardo speaks no English whatsoever. The process of describing my desired haircut, with the aid of hand gestures and pointing is a little disconcerting, but Eduardo, like a true pro, works it out. Freshly shorn, I load up the mountain bike, one rucksack on my back, one on my front in annoying Euro-backpacker style and slowly cycle down town to Penn station. I'm on the pavement in an attempt to avoid yellow cab-related mishaps. Suddenly I hear police sirens; I turn round: I'm being pulled over!? Fortunately for me the NYPD have better things to be doing, and I get let off with a warning. Much chastened I move onto the road and take my chances against the homicidal NYC cab drivers, while the magic bike creaks disconcertingly under the considerable weight of my backpacks.

Safely at Penn Station and I find that Amtrak is a pleasant and efficient way to travel; my bags are checked without hassle, my seat is both spacious and comfortable (about the size of a business class seat on an airplane) and strangest of all, the staff actually seem to enjoy their jobs, in stark contrast to their British counterparts. Only downside is a lack of choice in seat allocation, creating something of a travelling companion lottery. The ticket inspector is a huge African-American gentleman with a deep Barry White cadence. "Oh yeah" he rumbles as he slowly makes his way down the train: "Riding the Amtrak, time to contemplate, meditate, RELAX, oh yeah... what's that you got on your shirt there son? Hmmmn, ok then nice...." And so on. Full of optimism, I take a last look at New York as we slowly pull out of the station – it's leg one, and a mere twenty seven hours South to Miami.

The train rolls through familiar sounding cities; Philadelphia, Washington, and then suddenly through a neighbourhood that looks eerily familiar, even though I've never been here before. Row after row of semi-deserted streets and boarded up houses with their fading red paintwork, and weeds taking over. Suddenly I get it: this is Baltimore, setting for my all-time favourite show: 'The Wire'. I'm rapt at the window now, looking out for familiar streets and landmarks like some sort of twisted Disne world, but instead of Mickey and Goofy, there is a group of teenagers hanging around the street corners, approaching the slow moving cars. The misery is authentic enough though, and as the train slows to go under a graffiti covered bridge, emaciated homeless people lie motionless by the track side, and its genuinely difficult to tell if they are alive or dead. Ron, my current travel companion, a 60-something retired construction worker from Michigan, shakes his head: "These cities: Baltimore, Philly, Cleveland, they're dying, they're just dying. Twenty years from now and nobody will live here at all."

By evening we're into Virginia then the Carolinas. My travel companion now is Becky a tiny wee thing of indeterminate age. Young enough looking (and hugging a pink rabbit) to be a teenager, but with a world-weariness that suggests a longer and more storied life. Turns out to be the latter and in her few waking moments Becky divulges that she is in fact 27, a high school drop-out and mother to three children. None of whom are on the train. The rest of her back story seems to be nomadic and patchily dark; "Don't go to El-Paso, El-Paso really blows. Hard." Later on that night, I watch as Becky makes a painfully clumsy but determined attempt to pull the lounge car waiter. That explains the three kids then. By dawn we're in Savannah, Georgia before rolling slowly through Florida itself. Becky has disembarked and been replaced by Victoria, a 73 year old Jamaican woman who is perfectly lovely. Victoria has 5 children, 9 grandchildren and several great-grandchildren. She gently lectures me at length in soothing Jamaican tones on the importance of family, contentedness and the scourge that is racism. She also confesses a great desire to see the Queen one day ("Ooooh what a wonderful woman she is") but is so singularly unimpressed by my story about meeting Prince Philip that I decide not to launch into my impression of him. Probably for the best.

Back in the dinning car I meet Ron again- he's staring wistfully out of the window and nursing a cup of black coffee. He sees me and beckons me over and we fall into conversation. The long and steady rhythm of the rail road seems to soften people and make them open to talking-

I've already had more conversations with strangers on this train than all of my train journeys back home combined. I'm glad of the company too - Ron is an interesting man, but also incredibly melancholy. He's taking a break by himself - he has a little place in the Everglades with no phone reception, no internet and no neighbours. He says that much as he loves his family, he needs to get away from them and everybody else once in a while. Ron talks about a life spent in construction. Having spent a summer or two digging holes on building sites I can relate a little bit, although not to Ron's darker tales: "Yeah, I've seen all sort of things on site; seen a block of concrete land on a man, stuffed a rag in the hole where his head used to be…" Ron trails off and looks out the window, I can see his eyes going misty. In a nation obsessed with therapy Ron clearly comes from a time and place that isn't. Without it, I suspect that Ron will be carrying his ghosts for quite a while, probably for good, which is a damn shame if you ask me.

Finally, twenty seven hours later, the train pulls into Miami. By now I've developed a stinking cold. The heat and the humidity combine with this to make my head feel like it's going to explode. At my new hostel "Jazz on the Beach" in South Beach, I meet my new roomies, a group of young Eastern European girls, who have kindly decorated the room for my arrival by covering it in bikinis, bras and flip flops, and a charming German chap called Bern-heart (I think). I ask Annetta, the Eastern European girls' apparent leader, what they plan on doing tonight: She holds up a three litre bottle of Malibu and another of vodka: "We plan on doing this tonight." This doesn't bode well for my early night, that's for sure. They also plan on going clubbing, but the state of the local men is apparently something of a disappointment to the girls: "These men, hmmm, to me they are worse than gypsies ". Ah the casual racism of the young independent Eastern European traveller. Perhaps they'll fare better with Ollie, the final roomie. Ollie is quite clearly a product of the British Public School system and is unfailingly polite and well spoken. He is also disconcertingly pretty: I have dated women who were considerably less pretty than Ollie. Best not get too drunk, I decide. The girls in the room are already ruing the fact that the majority of the massive quantity of lotions and potions surrounding the sink actually belong to Ollie.

I wake early after a terrible night's sleep. The girls, somewhat predictably, fell into the bedroom at about 3am, totally smashed. My cold is also terrible and combined with a very short bed, sleep is somewhat broken. However, rising early, getting coffee and some of the strongest pharmaceuticals that the FDA will allow to be sold at the drugstore on the corner, and I'm feeling slightly better, and so take the bike out for a slow ride along ocean drive and Miami beach. Unfortunately, training is simply not on the agenda today, so I resign myself to having a lazy day of exploring and sunbathing instead. My magically unfolding mountain bike again garners appreciative nods and chatter from the Cuban cleaners and hostel goers, and I head out.

How best to describe Miami Beach. A brash, gross collection of God-ugly hotels, restaurants and palm trees soaked with oppressive heat, through which wander countless pairs of jiggling breasts. There are breasts everywhere. By 10am I'm actually feeling light headed, although maybe that's the pills kicking in. In the interest of balance, I should probably state that the place is also chock full of shirtless men sporting some of the most defined abs I've ever seen. There sure are a lot of breasts jiggling about the place though.

Miami Beach: the only thing that could possibly convince sane people to live in the sub-tropical swamp that is Florida. The beach is beautiful; the sand is clean and smooth, the water warm and clear, and the facilities plentiful. I splash around in the water for about an hour, and feel better for it, my head clearing a little bit. I stay at the beach till dark then had back to the hostel for dinner.

When human civilization finally breaks down, mealtimes will look something like this; a long queue of slightly dejected looking souls, waiting in line for the last of the rehydrated pasta, exchanged for a red coupon, all the while under the watchful eye of a muscle bound overlord, who ensures that the queue remains orderly, and nobody takes too much. I'm sure that after the fall the red coupon will have to be earned by working in a salt mine or the suchlike, but for now they can be purchased for five dollars at reception. Over dinner, one of the hostel guests, 'Patrick' is talking sports. Patrick is a student at

Miami University and is waiting for his apartment to come free. Patrick, it transpires, has played line-backer and has a 6-2 record as an amateur heavy-weight boxer. Tonight's discussion is on the subject of race in American Football, with Patrick contending that black players are useless quarterbacks, but great receivers. Most of the attending Brits take offence at the notion of race playing a role in sports. Patrick however is standing strong, and having both played football, and being black, brings his personal experience to the discussion:

Patrick: "Look man, I'm telling you, I played quarterback once"

British John: "Well there you go then, that proves it can be done. What happened?"

Patrick: "I sucked. Got replaced by a white dude."

Morning. My cold has started to clear and I feel in a considerably better mood for it. I decide to check out uptown to find the gym that belongs to Roberto 'Cyborg' Abreu. Cyborg, who earned his name when he was run over by a car and had to be re-built, is the number two no-gi grappler in the world at Super-Heavyweight, and a legitimate threat to the Gracie team's strangle hold on the World Championships. Cyborg made a name for himself when he suplexed man-mountain Jeff 'The Snowman'

Monson in a North-American wrestling tournament and he is known for sparring with his students regularly.

It takes me forty minutes to cycle to North beach, which only compounds my horror to find the fight-sports gym is shuttered up with a big 'for let' sign in the window. Distraught I head into the shop next door. Unfortunately this is little Brazil and the store owners speak little English. My attempts to sign "what happened to the gym next door?" elicit nothing but confused looks. In desperation I enquire "Cyborg?"

"Ahhhh, Cyborg! Si, Si, Si," followed by much pointing to the small Brazilian cafe across the street. I head over and after ordering an acai bowl (indescribable - you just have to try one) I enquire of the waiter if he knows what happened to the gym. "Oh you looking for the jiu-jitsu? Sure, they moved just a few doors down on the corner". I am much relieved. A few minutes later and the cafe phone rings. The waiter exchanges a few words in Portuguese then looks over at me and says "Hey man, Cyborg, he is coming..."

An intimidatingly large plate of food is put down at the seat next to me, and a few minutes later Cyborg himself walks through the door, exchanging handshakes, bear hugs, back-slaps and pleasantries with everyone in the place. Yes it seems like Cyborg is a big thing in little Brazil. Eventually he sits down. "Hello. My name is Jamie, I've come to train at your gym". "Heeeey, dats good man.

My name is Cyborg." I arrange to attend the Saturday open mat and the Monday morning training I leave Cyborg demolishing his overmatched plate of chicken.

Late afternoon: a volleyball game forms with six Brits. The standard of play is awful but the level of banter is high, possibly to the non-amusement of dog walking locals. It lacks both the athleticism and homo-eroticism of the 'Top-Gun' scene, but hey, we're playing volleyball on Miami Beach, and that has to be good enough. Back at the patio for drinks and Patrick rocks up, the first time he's been seen in nearly 24 hours. "Damn man, I just spent the night in jail". It transpires that Patrick went to a local sports bar, and accidentally trod on a man's foot (being at least 220lbs, it probably hurt). The man, according to Patrick, "Jacked me up," meaning that he grabbed Patrick by the shirt to remonstrate with him. At this point, Patrick dispensed with any further pleasantries and proceeded to hit the man in the head until club security removed both and called the police. Patrick spends the night in a holding cell with THIRTY other inmates. This provides much material for banter: "So, Patrick, did you, erm, meet anyone special in prison?" "Damn man, hell no, I didn't talk to nobody".

Later that night and a club trip is being organized by the hostel: entry to club 'MIA' and transport by limo and back all for ten dollars. This being Miami, and a Friday night, it seems like the right thing to do.

It isn't. Five minutes inside and I remember that I hate clubbing, and at $15 dollars a drink, taking the edge of with alcohol is not an option. Ordering a coke and ice (five dollars) the smiling bar-maid advises me: "You won't get there that way honey". She's not wrong. That leaves the music. Only drug-crazed robots could dance to this music; certainly not the squat muscle-men who shark the dance floor, the sugar daddies in the booths at the side nor the preening narcissistic women recording their every move on camera. And certainly not me. In the end it all just ends up looking like a heaving throng of sweaty humanity pressed into forced delirium. All of which means that clubbing is as bad in Miami as it is anywhere else. Limo or no limo.

Joining us in the club is my roomie Ollie, who, being only 18 years old, has been supplied with a spare i.d from another Brit traveller to whom he bears a passing resemblance. Clearly psyched to get in, and to be clubbing in Miami, Ollie finds his own solution to the drinks problem: he steals it. Around the dance floor there are many booths. In order to be allowed to sit in one of these booths you merely have to purchase a $400 bottle of vodka. These bottles are left in situ on the tables while the purchasers move around the club. Clearly nobody thinks that anybody would be foolish enough to simply steal any. They're wrong: Ollie is going great guns on the stuff. I gently try to explain to Ollie that whilst not everybody in this club is a gangster, not everybody isn't. He doesn't listen. Oh well, I decide that if he gets into trouble over this one he's on his own.

A few minutes later I've got problems of my own. A few feet away, one of the aforementioned squat muscle-men is having a domestic with his girlfriend. Things turn nasty and the man grabs her by the mouth and starts yanking her around. Not good. I've also just ordered a $15 glass of vodka cranberry and Patrick's recent experience with the law is running through my mind. But the man is not stopping. With a sigh and no small amount of trepidation I hand my drink to a Danish chap from the youth hostel and step forward. Thank God that at exactly that moment another man steps forward and the two of us manage to move the angry boyfriend backwards. Unfortunately, his girlfriend decides that this is now the appropriate juncture for retaliation and starts flailing her arms in his, and our, direction. Fearing that the whole thing is about to go South, I focus on trying to gently move her away from the situation. Undeterred, she keeps flailing with her talon-like fingernails. I end up with defence wounds on my hands for my troubles. Eventually, a huge bouncer appears and stands off, weighing the situation. Addressing him directly, I nod towards squat muscle man and state: "Him." The bouncer gives me the once over, nods and yanks the man towards the door. The woman is taken away by her friends and I retrieve my drink from a now stunned looking Dane and use at least $4 worth of high grade vodka to sterilize the cuts on my hands. Clubbing, pah.

Things pick up the following night. The hostel staff recommend 'Ted's hideaway,' a sports bar, stumbling distance from the hostel. A large European group, mostly Brits, and the omnipresent yet perennially skint Patrick, head out. There is no responsible way to drink beer this cheaply. $9 pitchers of Bud start to flow. The evening's highlights include Alex who looks the absolute spitting image of Jay from 'The Inbetweeners.' He tells me that he has been told of this similarity seven times on the holiday so far. "Go on, say clunge" I implore. Brilliantly, he does and lurches into a Jay impression so good that it hurts to laugh. Meanwhile the locals have a 'winner stays on' rule on the pool table. Too bad for them then, that our group includes British John, a classically trained snooker player from Sheffield. Two hours later John retires undefeated and lets the Americans have their table back. One of the other Brits, 'Big Ollie' makes the confession: "I was on the beach for two hours today and after two hours of consideration, I realised, I had the worst body on the entire beach."

Meanwhile, Inbetweener Tom and his travelling buddy Alex share their stories: Eighteen years old and just finished school, this pair of loveable backpacking halfwits are bussing it all around America on the Greyhounds, relying on good luck, English charm and the sense of total naïve indestructability that being eighteen years old brings. If you choose to travel on the Greyhound night-buses, you will need all of these qualities. Everybody who has ever been on one for more than an hour has a "Greyhound" story, and rarely a good one. The cheapest way to travel in America, the occupants of any given Greyhound bus probably pack enough firepower and

Thunderbird wine to be able to fight off a pack of marauding coyotes/vampires, should the bus break down in the middle of the New Mexican desert. Which is not, if we are being honest, completely out of the question. Several things are inadvisable when travelling the Greyhound. One is talking. The other is sleeping. Tom reveals that on one particularly hellish overnighter, a large Samoan gang kept staring intently at their rucksacks, and earnestly enquiring which stop they were getting off at. Tom and Alex adjusted to this threat by taking it in turns to sleep, and by padlock chaining their luggage to their legs. WG would probably have admired this pragmatic approach to transcontinental travel, but I'll stick with the luggage check on the Amtrak.

All said it was a fun night: British John pulls a remarkably hot barmaid, Patrick stays out of jail, and I just know that my head is going to hurt bad in the morning.

My head hurts. I have one full day left in Miami which I decide to spend on the beach, swimming in the sea as much as possible. Tomorrow I am heading out for the even hotter Houston to visit the Family Payne. It will be nice to stay in a place where you don't have to lock your valuables and take a chance on the toilet flush working. At least I hope that's how it will be. En route to the airport I will finally attempt to train with Cyborg. This will be cutting it fine though, and I hope that his time-keeping defies the Brazilian jiu-jitsu convention. If not, it's a heck of a long walk to Texas...

Miami Beach

All I can say is that it felt right in the context. Even though it wasn't.

Miami roomies and a sun-reflecting Englishman trying desperately to fit in.

Part III

I'll Shoot You and Your Lawyer

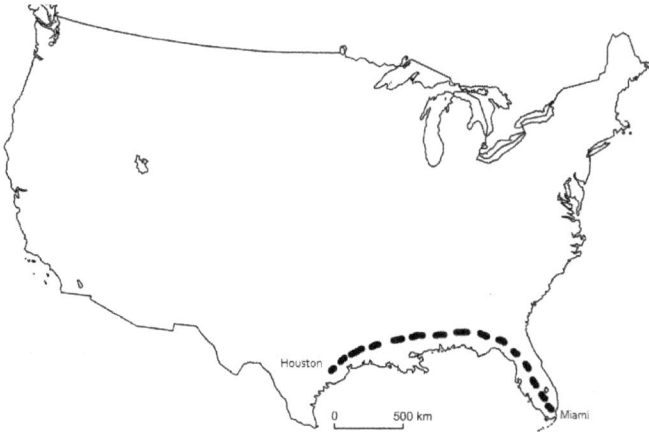

I left Miami in a whirl; on the last night the assembled youth hostel crowd made their way to a club actually on Miami beach. The club bristled with gang and pseudo gang menace, with no safe way to differentiate between the two. 'Inbetweener' Tom spent an improbable amount of time gamely chatting up a beautiful blonde woman at the bar. She's garbed in thigh high black boots, fish nets, A-line skirt and pig-tails. Judging by her total lack of female or male company in the club, the slightly more world-weary travellers conclude that she is almost certainly a very high class prostitute. Or maybe just a well-dressed one. At any rate, Tom's chances are slim at best, and after a while, fellow Brits: Big Ollie, Lee and I head for the beach proper where we chew the fat till sun up. At daybreak I take a slow walk back to the hostel in the cool dawn of a Miami morning, say my goodbyes, then it's off to Houston Texas to stay with the Family Payne- my long suffering friend and part-time travel agent Stuart, Gill his wife, Matthew (age 3) and Georgia (age 6), the latter of whom also happens to be my God-daughter. I met Stuart when we lived together in first year at University. Little has changed little since then except that instead of hanging out in Stuart's spare armchair (he would argue that as it was his only armchair it wasn't really spare) I am hanging out in a spare wing of his house. Also, he is married, has two children and is vice-president of a major oil company. So I guess that some things have changed, but fundamentally the dynamic of our relationship remains.

I cheat, and take a flight from Miami. Unfortunately, due to the destruction wrought by hurricane Katrina there is simply no sensible way to travel to Houston from Florida by train; the only route takes you through both Washington and Chicago, and lasts 67 hours. To make up for this I informed Stuart of my intention to cycle from the airport to his house, some 14 miles. Stuart informs me that I will do no such thing. The journey would involve a short stretch on an eight lane mega-highway, where anything smaller than a pick-up is little more than moving road-kill, and Stuart has no intention of informing my mother that I am now deceased due to a cultural mis-understanding involving my bike, an interchange and a sixty-ton truck. It's true that despite the optimistic amount of cycle lanes, I don't see a single soul using them during my short stay in Houston. So two hours and an uneventful flight later, I'm in Houston and playing about with Matthew and Georgia in the friendly, and very, very safe, ex-pat gated community of White Oaks. Woodie Guthrie, passing this way in the thirties, wrote that Houston was full of nothing but flop houses and pot smokers. Things have changed- Houston, although considered something of a liberal enclave in an otherwise highly conservative state, is now the oil capital of America, if not the whole world.

It's hot here, but it's not the sweltering heat of Miami Beach. Although in Miami I didn't have a two stone hat of one Matthew; who has decided that being carried around on my shoulders is just about the only way to travel.

After a week in a pretty ratty youth hostel, I'm relieved to be in a king sized bed. The bed would be big enough for a particularly self-indulgent king, with a predilection for personal space. Still, as I will shortly come to learn, everything is big in Texas.

On my first full day, Stu has kindly taken the day off work, and we set out for what will transpire to be the manliest day of my life so far. In the morning we head for one of Houston's many shooting ranges, where we are both booked in for a lesson in handgun shooting. On arrival we are greeted, with no small amount of suspicion, bordering on open hostility, by 'Hank', the range owner. Now I don't actually know Hank's real name, but as I don't really like him, Hank will do just fine. After brief and uncomfortable introductions we are assigned a teacher, a young man of Asian descent who is friendly, polite, helpful and intelligent. He knows all about UK gun laws having written essays on the subject for his degree course. After a short intro on firearm safety (the brevity of which clearly has Stu worried - no power points either) we stride out confidently to the range. We are given our choice of handgun from their considerable armoury. After a little browsing in the redneck equivalent of a pick 'n' mix, Stu opts for the Glock 17, which happens to be the standard issue firearm for UK police armed officers. Not for me however: I'm in Texas and I want a revolver. So I get the Ruger snub nosed double action SP101 which fires .38 specials, a considerably higher caliber than Stu's 9mm, although it lacks the capacity and rapid rate of fire.

After one box of ammo the jury is back in: I LOVE GUNS, and intend to write to my MP immediately upon my return requesting the repeal of all gun controls. Texas will do that to you. I'm pleased to say that both Stu and I give a good account of ourselves, offering some reasonably accurate shooting, and nobody killed. After about half an hour of mindless fun, our teacher comes back and says; "So you guys look ok, do you want to have a go with something a bit bigger?" Do tell, my friend. Back in the armory and we survey the range of fire-power that the state of Texas will legally allow us to play with. I nearly go for a long barreled Smith and Weston .47 special, but when our teacher utters the word 'Uzi'…well, you get the idea.

Now, not even the state of Texas is foolhardy enough to simply give me a fully automatic machine gun. So after my driving licence has been seized, and I've signed a photocopy proclaiming that I am neither a felon or a mental, I'm escorted to the range, where the teacher carries the UZI, loads the UZI and then hands the UZI to me. At this point I am ready to go. I am given a choice of target. Let's see, Zombie, Osama Bin Laden, Zombie Osama Bin Laden? Winner. In the next booth, a Texan local, is disturbed by the sound of automatic fire, and comes round to see. While I am happily blasting away, he turns to Stu and enquires:

"UZI?"

"Yep"

"Fuuuuuuuuckkkkk".

I finish my 200 rounds and both teacher and Texan local seem surprised and impressed by my tight grouping; Zombie Bin-Laden no longer has a head. Yes, the UZI is a truly ridiculous weapon: Not enough range to use as a rifle, not enough accuracy to be used for law enforcement, the UZI really is only good if you are quite definite in wanting to kill the man in front of you and aren't too bothered about killing the man behind him. The local seems buzzed: "Damn, I didn't even know you could get one of dem'. Well, heck, you boys have fun now", before leaving, shaking his head with a huge grin. I suspect it will not be long before the great state of Texas has another UZI owner.

Less fun are the intermittent conversations that we have with Hank. Hank is about fifty, bearded, and an opinionated fool. Hank is also very angry: angry with the President, do-gooders, liberals and the 'love-your-neighbour-types,' whom Hank states he would love to see over the top of his gun barrel. This is how Hank speaks: in nonsensical nuggets that he's gleaned from bumper stickers and t-shirts. It's hard to tell how much of this is bravado for the foreign outsiders who are his audience, and how much is genuine, but his anger at the perceived forces aligned to restrict his freedom to shoot whatever the hell he wants is very real. Hank also seems angry at us; annoyed that a rare chance to rail at liberal foreigners is being spiked by our politeness, willingness to learn and, in my case at least, a reasonable history and aptitude with guns. All this is a shame, because the other staff and patrons here are friendly and helpful. They are eager to pass on their knowledge and obvious enthusiasm for shooting and seem pleased at our obvious enthusiasm for learning. They are, in short, a walking argument for responsible gun ownership. In sharp contrast with Hank, who in his paranoid, angry and ridiculous outbursts (see the title of this chapter) is not an argument against guns, he's just an asshole, plain and simple. I'm glad his influence stretches no further than the shredded tires that make up his shooting range. And that he probably doesn't have a passport.

In the evening Stu and I go for dinner at "Taste of Texas," a high-end local steak house. Now, I am a vegetarian, a vegetarian who occasionally goes nuts on Sushi, but a vegetarian nonetheless. But this is Texas, and there is no vegetarian option. So I decide to give myself a pass. Now, when most vegetarians slip, they normally end up with a bacon roll. Not for me. I'm slipping on a 32 ounce Porter House steak. Holy hell. Our waiter takes us to the kitchen to discuss our favoured cut with the house butcher, then takes us back to the table where he has a 'surprise' for me: being a first timer at TofT, he ties a bright red bandanna round my neck, thus making me "an honorary Texan" for the night. Or a burk in a bandanna, depending on your view. Over dinner Stuart explains a little bit about the Texan obsession with freedom. "Look, take washing machines - there's no lock on the door. That's deliberate. As far as the average Texan is concerned, they paid for the washing machine, they own the washing machine, and if they want to open the door in the middle of the cycle and flood their home, well that's a matter of personal freedom. Try to take that freedom by putting a lock on the door, and you might as well let the terrorists win and join a kibbutz..."

After some pretty heavy eating, I managed to finish. As Stu later comments: "I threw down the gauntlet. And you ate it." Nearby there is a place that serves a 64 ounce steak: a plaque on the wall and a photo in the local rag awaits those up to the challenge. Apparently some have died trying. On the way out of the restaurant I pause to wrestle with a grizzly bear. At Stuart's behest, and when there's no waitresses watching, I also pause to pose for a picture of me being sodomized by the same bear. It's just been one of those days.

The following morning and its wrestling for real: I'm booked in for a 1-1 training session with 'Reed,' a former state high school wrestling champion. Looking through his resume, I reckon that he would probably walk straight onto the British National team, if not the Olympics, such is the relative paucity of our much faded wrestling tradition compared to the US, where the ability to pile another human male through the floor is still good enough to get you a pretty decent college education for free. However, America is full of young men who, having put themselves through years of physical abuse, for no money and little recognition outside the wrestling world, end up as very, very good wrestlers, but not quite good enough to make the Olympics, and secure the limited financial support that is available post-college. At this juncture the wrestler is faced with stark choices: there are simply not that many avenues where a killer power-double leg is a sought after attribute. The options are limited to teaching, professional prize fighting, or in many cases, both. Gill is worried that I haven't eaten any breakfast; knowing how hard wrestlers train, I'm worried that I've eaten too much. Fortunately, Reed has in mind a slow technical session, patiently running through wrestling basics and correcting the mistakes that I've been making for years. At the end we spar. Reed could blatantly crush me like a grape, but chooses not to. Even so after two minutes my lungs are burning, and I get an appreciation for just how hard top level wrestlers train.

Gill and Matthew pick me up from the gym and it's onto downtown Houston for lunch and a walking tour. Down town Houston turns out to be mostly underground: 7 miles of underground tunnels that Houstonians use to get out of the heat. But it does leave above ground almost eerily quiet and business like. Later, back at the house, Georgia is back from school and wants to go for a run. I'm sure that the neighbours think I'm running slow for Georgia's sake: I'm not- it is very, very hot in Houston in the afternoon.

The following morning, Stuart and I go a popular chain restaurant that specializes in pancakes. Much like cigarettes there is simply no safe way to consume this company's products. They don't even pretend to have a healthy option. To my liking however, is the coffee that arrives in a flask bigger than my head.

Friday. After a fun and restful week, it's time to go - I'm heading West on the train, all the way to Los Angeles and the Pacific Ocean. It has been good to see the Family Payne and I feel rested ahead of my 47 hour journey to California. All in all, I like Texas, certainly more than Miami. It's good to get a little insight into the Southern mindset, detached form the gun-toting- red-neck stereotypes that pervade the media. That said, if any foreign power is ever foolish enough to attempt to invade America, they would be well advised to leave Texas until last. Or just go around it.

Wildly inaccurate, but fun as hell all the same

Steak, Texas style.

Bear wrestling.

Part VI

Mountain Time

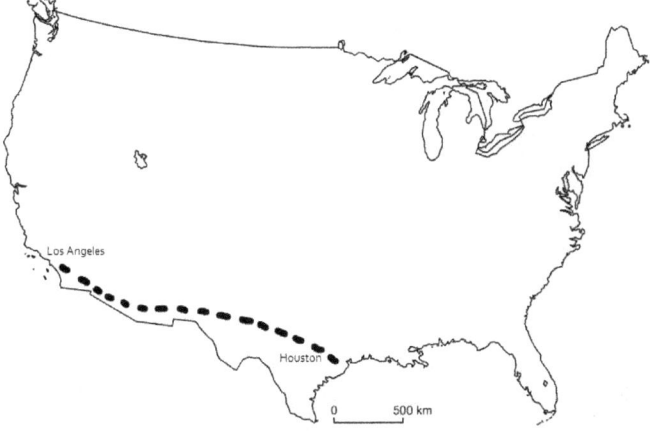

It's late when I leave Houston. Stu has arranged for a driver, Joseph, to take me to the station, which is housed in a less than salubrious part of town. Joseph and I talk for the twenty minute trip - he's never been to London and is keen to hear about it. As we pull into the Station yard, Joseph's cool demeanour shifts some, and he looks nervous. As we unpack my bags he looks about warily, and bids me a safe trip. As I head inside I note that he doesn't get back into the car until I'm safely talking to the Station Guard, which is nice.

I'm riding the Sunset Limited 'Superliner:' A huge double-decker train that is even better equipped than the one that took me from New York to Miami. I have a massive double seat to myself at the rear of the train, and as the lights are dimmed the various travellers settle themselves down to sleep. All, except the party three rows in front of me that is. Fat, loud, drunk and obnoxious, they board at Houston and are travelling through to San Antonio. They shout loudly in a mangled ugly bastardisation of the English language: "Who da hell be sleeping? Ain't nobody on dis coach, dat's fur damn sure..." They proceed to amuse themselves by singing. Not songs mind, but the jingles from their favourite adverts, most of which seem to be for hotdogs. To give a gauge of their ability, they try to sing 'Row your boat' but forget the words half way through the first verse. Fortunately, by 2.am we have reached San Antonio- they disembark, and the train rolls peacefully out of town and into the darkness of the Texan desert. I drift off and sleep for hours.

Dawn, and I wake to see the sun rising over the desert. The conductor makes an announcement that the lounge car is now open for coffee. I doze for a while taking in the landscape. The train slips slowly through the vast stretch of scrub, populated by a few cattle. Three cowboys sit on the hood of a truck watching the train go by. They actually wave to the train as we pull slowly past them. I wave back.

Breakfast in the restaurant car is a pleasingly sumptuous affair. The omelette I order is freshly cooked and huge. Best of all, the coffee is free and refillable. I'm seated with Ralph, a retired landscape gardener of about 70, and his sister, who have been travelling Texas to see family and are now headed back to Nevada. Ralph is quietly spoken and surprisingly knowledgeable about British current affairs, amongst many other subjects. Ralph is pleased to learn that I am a public servant and that my twin-brother, a Captain in the army, has recently got back from serving with the Americans in Afghanistan, and he thanks us both for our service, which gets to me a little. We talk for an hour and a half, breaking to watch the Rio Grande pass on the left hand side, and beyond it, Mexico. Ralph reflects on the immigration issue, and confesses a deep respect for the travails of the border jumpers, in contrast to a laziness and lack of work ethic he sees back home. Eventually we are cleared from the restaurant car so they can ready for lunch. Ralph gives me his details, assuring me that we have much still to talk about, and that he will stay in touch with me. He means it too.

Lunchtime passes and the train pulls into the small town of 'Alpine,' Texas. The conductor announces that this will be a cigarette break, meaning that I have a few minutes to step out and stretch my legs. Alpine doesn't even have a Station house, let alone a platform, and as the door opens I step out on the gravel next to the tracks, then walk a short way to a low wooden fence, sit, and take in the scene. Alpine seems to have two roads, a main street and a second that fades out after a couple of hundred yards into the bush, disappearing into the scrub and rocks. At least the person who named it had a sense of humour. It's hot and so I get some shade next to the train and chat to Thomas, the conductor. Alpine, it transpires, is popular with artists and the like, doubtless drawn in by the dramatic mountains to the North and what I am quite sure will be reasonably priced housing. Soon enough, a whistle goes, and the smokers, stretchers and gawkers re-board, and the train continues its way West, into what my friend Lucy used to call "album cover America."

Sitting in the café car, a young mother, with a very clear voice reads to three young children a history of the Roman Empire. I have to confess that she reads so well that I am captivated, and am only pretending to read my newspaper, while actually listening to story time. Looking round, I strongly suspect that I am not alone in this. The Romans invented books? Who knew?

Late afternoon and the vistas have opened up into huge open expanses with great rolling clouds over sparse, arid red sand. Sitting in my carriage I can see Mexico on my left as we skirt just next to the border, and to my right, we have left Texas and moved into New Mexico, marked by the impressive Franklin mountains. Woodie Guthrie knew this country well. So did Jack Kerouac; riding out West with Dean Cassidy in a doomed attempt to find God in the endless horizons. I kick back and put on some Johnny Cash. The conductor makes an announcement: "We are now on Mountain Time, if your cell phone is not on Mountain Time, it's broken: throw it away and get a new one..."

The day draws on, and by evening we are leaving New Mexico and crossing into Arizona. By 10PM we pull into Tucson, where we will have a cigarette break for an hour. I take the chance to leave the train and cross the street into the nearest bar. I realize quickly that it is a pretty swanky place, and after 36 or so hours on a train, in a grey t-shirt and flip flops, I am not exactly dressed (or washed) for the occasion. No matter, the hostess has no problem with finding me a seat at the bar. The strapping barman, with a ridiculously deep voice, recommends a local brew: "Rogue Dead Guy Ale." Well, with a name like that, it would be impossible to say no. Turns out that RDGA packs a mighty punch, and after half a pint I'm feeling dizzy. I finish and make to pay. The barman waves me off: "No Boss, that'll be on me, boss." I have no idea what I've done to deserve a pint on the house, but you have to like a town where, after half an hour, the local barman is buying you a beer, and a good one at that. I offer my hand, then make my way back to the train and another night travelling through the desert.

Morning. I wake up to be confronted by the face of a very small Hispanic child staring intently at me. This is a disconcerting way to start the morning, especially as I don't remember a small Hispanic child on the seat next to me when I fell asleep. Fortunately the mother of said child, who is one seat over, wakes up and reclaims her progeny. It transpires that they boarded sometime over the night, while I was sleeping off the RDGA.

California. It's sunny and we are pulling into the outskirts of LA. Hopefully we will keep on pulling, because I for one have no intention of disembarking in this neighbourhood, which features the scariest graffiti I've seen since visiting Belfast. Woody Guthrie wrote that if he was starving in LA and somebody gave him a nickel, he would use it to buy a bus ticket out. I arrive at the Grand Central Station and find my bus. The driver doesn't have change for a five dollar bill, and just waves me on for free. On board it's crowded as hell, but I don't care; we zip along towards Santa Monica and the coast. After a long ride, I hop out and unfurl my bike. Climbing on with both rucksacks, I free wheel it down to the youth hostel, and just beyond, the Pacific Ocean. As Kerouac put it; "We can't go any further- cos' there ain't no more land."

Prairie country, somewhere in Texas

Sunset, New Mexico

65

Interlude: Swimming in New-Age Soup

In my head, my journey was going to take me all around the American border. I've made it to the West Coast, but I've come to a stop in LA, still a little North of the Mexican Border. Really I should have turned South at this point and made it all the way down to San Diego, the most southerly city in Southern California. But I've checked the map and my schedules and there is just no way; I'd barely have time to turn around before I'd be back on a train and back tracking North in an attempt to make it to Seattle on time. So I'm not going, but I'd hate for you, the reader, to miss out, so here is a brief interlude from when I did make it to San Diego, for a short trip two years ago. It was the end of a miserable British winter, and the allure of the golden beaches, not to mention some of the best jiu-jitsu on the planet, was just too much to take. I think that it's important to include it here, because you really should be aware of the risks of eating a giant fish burrito before you try one. I did, so you don't have to.

San Diego, February 2009

I arrived at the Ocean Beach Hostel at about midnight Monday, having been awake for some 46hours, a new record for me. Admittedly some sleep on the plane, just enough to allow me to get through border control looking vaguely sane (which is more than could be said for the border guard). For some reason, known only to the international airline industry, the cheapest way to get from London to San Diego is via Minnesota. I'm used to landing in JFK, which makes the 'Twin Cities Airport' look like a bit of a backwater. The arrivals hall is spookily empty (where have all the other passengers gone?) and the carpet is the sort of psychedelic patterning that was inexplicably popular in the 70's. Gingerly, I make my way up to the immigration booth. The old, heavily moustached guard looks me over and examines my passport forensically. "Soooooo" he says, a touch dramatically, "Tell me a story, watcha doing here?" "Well Sir, (always best to call them sir, I find) I'm heading down to San Diego for a two week holiday". He looks up "Really? I'm from San Diego originally" "Oh, really?" I reply, trying to sound enthusiastic. "Nope, just something I like to tell people." I decide that it's time to get out of the airport- my passport safely stamped I make my way to the exit. I've got six hours to kill before my connecting flight. Picking up a free map and contemplating what to do in a city that I've barely heard of and will almost certainly never return to, I look at my options. The "Mall of America" is a short bus trip away. My free map, which I suspect receives some form of financial support from said Mall, informs me that it is the highlight of any trip to the twin cities. Well, let me save you the time if you should ever happen this way: its shit. True enough, it is massive, indeed the biggest in America, but really: how many Gap/Starbucks/etc do you need in one place? Looking again at my map I search from an alternative: looks like the Mississippi river is a few blocks away. For the next hour I walk through empty streets until I reach the Ol' Man River itself. Yep, just like the Mall of

America, it is very big. I stand by the banks and stare for a few minutes. About 800 miles downstream of where I'm standing, Jeff Buckley walked into this river, fully clothed, and was never seen again. I take a solitary photo and walk back to the airport.

Border control weirdness and one big river later and I'm on a connecting flight and make it into San Diego and the Ocean Beach hostel without incident. I pass out on arrival and sleep for a few hours, but my body clock has no idea what is going on now, and kindly wakes me at 6am. Oh well. Unsurprisingly the hostel is silent and empty at this time. I walk out past the dozing night guard and onto the main street. It's just getting light, the palm trees are blowing gently in the wind. I look right - nothing but a long straight street. I look left and there it is: The Pacific Ocean, about a hundred yards from the front door. Stopping at the 24 hour mart, I pick up some water, tooth paste and brush and a cup of coffee. I wander down to the beach and sit on a stone sea wall, and look out at the ocean while giving me teeth a long over-due clean. Then there's nothing to be done but watch the sun-up and drink the oh-so-strong black coffee. Sheer bliss, these little moments.

Back at the hostel and it's time for breakfast. I am amused to discover that this place is less of a passing point for international backpackers and more of a flop house for Americans to lay low while they sort out their various legal issues. Thrown into the mix are the usual blend of amorous Frenchmen, drunken Aussies, and the requisite number of attractive European female backpackers. I made it to breakfast first thing where I meet an original hippie from San Francisco of the 60's who described herself as being 'between residences.' She was complaining of a headache and despite seemingly having taken every drug known to man, and some that aren't, she had never heard of the ibuprofen I offered her. Later at breakfast a slightly scary mature woman introduced herself, explaining that she was looking for work and a new place to live. Which I think essentially makes her a bum. Given the amount of attention and fixed stares she has been giving me of late I think she may be under the impression that I am going to sleep with her.

I am not going to sleep with her.

Later on I took the time to explore Ocean Beach, which is the area I'm staying in. It had its hay-day in the summer of love and has stubbornly refused to move on since then. Its faded appearance looks like something out of the Lost Boys film. The shops are strictly locally owned, with the sole exception of a Starbucks that prompted street protests when it opened two years ago. The shops cater to the tourist market and feature the authentically hippie-thrift shops and the like, and the in-authentically hippie, selling such nonsense as hemp rope sandals and organic incense. Naturally, the large number of genuine hippies and beach-bums who populate this neighbourhood cannot afford to shop in these establishments but show their support for local business through prolific shoplifting. This has prompted something of a backlash and most shops contain placards warning of dire, dire consequences for would be thieves. My personal favourite was found in a clothes shop, where the owner had placed a sign up under the title "Anger." It stated the following:

"Anger? You want to see me angry? Try stealing from me. I'll be so god damn angry you won't believe it; I'll beat the crap out of you then take your photo and post it in all the local papers with the word "thief" underneath it. STOP STEALING MY SHIT".

In the diner next door to the hostel, a good place to get breakfast when you've had enough of hostel porridge, there is a large sign reading: "No Snivelling".

This holiday is all about the training and exercise for me. I am not going to be distracted by girls this time. The training itself is going well. I'm at the "Throwdown Elite Training Centre;" a full time MMA gym chock full of friendly but ultra-aggressive wrestlers. The quality of the instruction is world-class; yesterday's session began with the instructor stating that "Today we are going to learn the 'super-unstoppable-guard-pass-of-death." Chief instructor at the Throwdown, is one Dean Lister, at one time the world's best jiu-jitsu fighter and 'Ultimate Fighting Championship' middleweight contender. Given this, it is surprising how low key the guy is. The warm up is normally well underway before Dean emerges from the changing room and slips onto the back of the matted area, hoodie pulled up and clutching a can of the Throwdown's patented energy drink. Dean sits on the mat watching the students perform cartwheels, bunny hops and the usual plethora of exhausting BJJ warm up techniques before slowly rising, polishing off the last of the energy drink and announcing "Ok, today we're going to look at half-butterfly guard sweeps to back-mount…"

Ah yes, energy drinks. America has an admirable range of high energy drinks that make red-bull look like Horlicks. The drinks companies seem to be in an arms race to make the first beverage that will kill you dead with one single serving . Currently out in the lead is Monster, who have discarded the tactic of ever-increasing caffeine quotas and simply made their can three times the size of everybody else's. They even have a specially constructed 'big gulp' opening to allow you to pour the toxic brew straight down your gullet. The good folks at monster are at least taking their social responsibility seriously by issuing advice not to drink more than two cans per day. That's not more than two litres of monster. I'm currently sticking with "Amp - an intense burst of energy." That'll be sugar then.

Back in Ocean Beach and eating revolves around choosing from the various fast food outlets, entirely owned by Mexicans whose English is about on a level with my Spanish. The food is all authentically Mexican. Authentic Mexican food makes me nostalgic for a plate of nachos from Wetherspoons or some Old El Paso from

Tesco. For the uninitiated here is my quick guide to Mexican food:

Enchiladas: A Flour tortilla swimming in slop.

Burrito: A Flour tortilla containing slop.

Taco: A flour tortilla with slop falling out of it.

Quesadilla: Two flour tortillas squashed together (contains slop).

More multi lingual fun was to be had at one of the hostel's nightly parties, where I was befriended by a very unpleasant Frenchman, who decides to bless me with his thoughts on the various girls in the hostel:

(With thick drunken French accent) "Oh my friend those Belgian girls are so hot. I would like to fuck one in the face..."

Meanwhile the mature woman from breakfast still seems to be under the impression that I am going to sleep with her. I am not going to sleep with her.

Last night the partying reached new heights with a weekly beach party, featuring vodka shots, and a fun game of avoiding being seen by the local constabulary while holding an open container of alcohol. A big bonfire, a Spanish guitar playing troupe and a silly amount of flavoured vodka - the fault of a nice German girl called Diana. Sat on the sand next to me, my long-haired hostel friend Les appears to have had several vodka shots too-many and on this cloudless Southern-Californian night is swaying to the rhythms in his head while communicating with the cosmos. He's probably got the right idea- watching the waves break on the shore and looking at the enormity of the Pacific Ocean, it's not difficult to understand what bought the hippies here in the first place: walk into that Ocean and swim in a straight line and you wouldn't hit land for thousands of miles, and by then you'd be in the southern islands of Okinawa.

I eventually stumbled home to the hostel but not before I managed to make a total arse out of myself. From what I remember, I hugged a homeless man, gave alcohol to another and worse of all was discussing hip hop with a local rap group who were doing an impromptu display of "flow" for the assembled crowd. Head of this troupe is a man who introduces himself as "Green Hex". Brilliant. Our conversation is interrupted when a young and frankly very square French tourist decides to step up and interrupts one of Green Hex's rapping partners with a rap of his own. I'm not 100% but he appears to be 'dissing' Green Hex. Even a rap neophyte like me knows that this is probably a bad idea. After all, I've seen '8 Mile' and I'm pretty sure it was a cautionary tale. Green Hex looks unimpressed and interrupts French rapper with a beautifully paced set of rhymes deconstructing the limitations of French rap and his adversary's choice of haircut. It's brilliant. French rapper looks crestfallen and disappears into the crowd and Green Hex returns to our conversation. Our conversation lasts some time, which is surprising as I don't know anything about rap. Thank god I didn't try to join in. At least I think I didn't but it all gets pretty hazy around that point.

The following morning and I am feeling very much worse for wear. I mean really, drinking that much vodka was a silly idea, spectacularly executed. I give myself a day off training as the idea of being squashed under an improbably muscular wrestler called Brian really doesn't do it for me today. My sloth lasts to the afternoon when a hostel sports game is organised. The Americans insist on calling this game "soccer". Call it what you want though, they still can't play it for shit. It's four-a-side. Opposing me is a team of four Americans. On my team: a Frenchman, an Argentinean and a Brazilian. Even with the drag factor of having me in goal the Americans get a damn good drubbing. I myself score a header for the first time since 1996, much to the delight of my teammates and proceed to celebrate this by doing the pull-your-t-shirt-over-your-head and run around stupidly bit. This is fine up to the point when I tread on a fucking bee and get stung in the foot thus ending my sporting endeavours much to the amusement of all.

On the way back to the hostel I see a bumper sticker that reads: "God bless America. Except Idaho. Fuck Idaho."

Enjoying a long afternoon siesta I'm disorientated to wake and find five very pretty French girls are now occupying my room. This is the sort of thing that does not happen in my house. If nothing else this leads to a fine face-book profile picture that demonstrates the joy of hostelling more than any travel guide could ever do. Things grow darker later when one of the aforementioned French girls nearly manages to burn down my bunk bed with a pair of hair straighteners with me still in it. And I've not been able to get into the bathroom since they arrived. Which is ok as I suspect the hot water has long since departed.

Training continues to go well, although I am disturbed at the number of men who do not shower after each session, which considering you are exchanging sweat with at least half a dozen other people is fairly disgusting. A nasty skin infection can't be too far off.

Always keen to fit into local customs and practices, I decide to go surfing. All week I've seen a young Japanese chap coming and going, always wearing a wetsuit and carrying a surf board under his arm. Travelling alone like me, he devotes almost every waking hour to surfing. Chatting to him over breakfast I learn that the surf is most definitely up. The hostel promptly lends me a surfboard for ten dollars and I'm all set. Strolling to the beach on a sunny San Diegan morning I'm full of enthusiasm- after all I'm no first time surfer. Three years previous I took a week off work, drove down to Cornwall and spent my time taking lessons on Fistral beach from a tassel haired Australian who insisted on calling me "Big Dude". Armed with this experience and British pluck, I wade into the waters.

Twenty minutes later I realize that all is not going as planned. Never mind catching a wave, never mind standing up, I can't even manage to haul my sorry-self onto the hulking lump of fiberglass. The currents are strong and the waves keep crashing down on me- no sooner have I managed to pull myself into a prone position on the board, than another wave has blasted me straight back off again, leaving me quite literally hanging on for dear life. After nearly an hour I'm no closer to recapturing my surfing glory, something that has clearly been outrageously enlarged in my own mind. I am however, exhausted, and deciding that drowning while tied to an unsightly lump of blue fiberglass is an undignified way to go, I admit defeat and doggy paddle my way back to the shore. After a couple of minutes of hard work I'm back on dry land and collapse in a heap on the sand. Having caught my breath I sit up and see two surfer girls staring at me. "Aww, first time?" enquires one, with apparently genuine concern. "Sort of - it's a bit different here" I reply. Christ I feel like a tool.

Undeterred by my surfing failure, and determined to experience so-cal culture, I decide to buy a skateboard. It seems like everybody skates in the OB, even a postman who I saw delivering mail yesterday. Over breakfast I discuss the issue with my hostel friends Les and Dan. Now Les has long hair and Dan says 'rad' a lot, so I figure they know what they are talking about. Fully briefed on skateboard consumer advice I grab a coffee to-go and walk the five blocks to where the local surf and skate shop is located. En-route I pass a small wooden white-washed chapel. On the side of the chapel is what looks like a mailbox, but next to it is a pad, a pen and a sign that reads: "Need prayer? Drop us a note". Nice, but hopefully not necessary.

Its ten thirty in the morning by the time I find the shop, but I'm the only customer to be seen. The only worker, a middle-aged woman with a deep tan and frizzy sea-air hair is hunched over a surf board, applying some sort of treatment to it and totally oblivious to my presence. The shop smells of gluc, and standing next to the counter the women still hasn't noticed me. On closer nasal examination of the odor it becomes apparent why: this woman is completely and totally baked. After a few more moments she looks up and sees me over the surf board. Removing her face mask she says "Ohhhhh, heeeeeyyy there, didn't see ya". I explain that I am there to purchase my first skateboard: "all-right- far-outtttt…"

I am directed to the second hand section and spend some time browsing through the battered and beaten 'decks' attempting to find one that has big-wheels; the sum total of Dan's advice. Eventually I settle on a 'gravity' board, apparently a local company. Well, I'm always keen to support local businesses. I part with my forty dollars and leave the shop to be confronted with a road that I swear didn't look so busy and intimidating just a few minutes previously.

Obviously I can't actually skateboard-for-toffee, so much of the day is taken up by half-assed attempts to stand on it and not look too much of a dick. Neither one of these things is easy and my efforts elicit no small number of smiles from the amused locals. I can report that skateboarding is nowhere nearly as easy as it looks. I am now engaged in an activity where pebbles can prove fatal. After several embarrassing prat-falls in public I retreat to the quiet residential back streets to practice. Settling on a street with no pedestrians, no traffic and a long and gentle decline, I hop on the board, my eyes scouring the near distance for signs of cracked pavement slabs, drains, pebbles or any other minor aberration that can now equal humiliation and slight bruising. Things are going well - too well: the decline may be gentle by in no time at all I've built up quite a speed and realize that I have no idea at all how to stop, or even decrease speed. Looking ahead I see that a busy intersection awaits me and I am forced to contemplate the most humiliating possible end to my life since the time I got lost on a night time jog around a golf course and seriously had to entertain the prospect of 'digging-in' till day light to avoid hyperthermia. With my options dwindling I start looking for escape routes. Up ahead I spot a front garden with lush green grass that appears both comfortable and traffic free. With perfect timing I leap off the board and enjoy a soft, injury free landing. My skateboard rides on majestically into the distance, unbothered by its sudden unburdening. Picking myself up I realize the whole sorry debacle has been witnessed by a woman sat in a deck chair in what I can only assume is her front garden. "Good morning" I say, with as much nonchalance as I can muster. She doesn't say anything so I quietly slope off to look for my skateboard. I catch up with it a couple of hundred yards further down the hill, where it has safely come to rest in a ditch. I have yet to work out how to fit my new purchase into my luggage, or indeed, if I should at all.

Meanwhile, back at the hostel, things have got darker; the lovely French identical twins and their equally lovely friends have departed, doubtless to be replaced by farting Australians. Having proven unsuccessful in courting said French girls, my Liverpudlian room-mate and new friend Dan confesses the truth about the 'cheeky chappie Liverpudlian' chat up technique:

"It never fucking works. Ever".

The partying is getting darker too; at the twice weekly beer pong party, the scary mature woman performed an impromptu lap dance in my face. It was not pleasant. I didn't know where to look, although I certainly knew where not to. When she starts taking her clothes off I make my excuses and move, only to have my head grabbed by an Irish girl with improbably sized breasts who proceeds to thrust them into my face and 'jiggle.' Dazed, confused and somewhat violated I retreat for the relative sanity of the street. At least when the beach-bum hippies accost you for money they hardly ever take their clothes off.

Tuesday. Today is Saint Patrick's Day and the majority of people on the streets are clad in at least one green item of clothing. The Irish girls in the hostel started drinking at nine, only slightly later than the resident alcoholics. The celebrations in Ocean Beach tonight promise to be messy. Meanwhile, Brian, my skateboard savvy friend, is heading out to get a tattoo of a camel. On his toe.

My head hurts. This is the result of a bout of drinking loosely inspired by St Patrick's Day. Considering that Mexicans outnumber the Irish in Ocean Beach by at least 20-1 and hippies outnumber both by an even greater factor, St Patrick 's Day seems to be taken very seriously here. Keen to avoid being pinched all night, the penalty for not being suitably attired, I go out to buy an item of green clothing. Sadly, all the bums have already emptied the thrift stores of any reasonably sensible green shirts and I am forced to spend eight dollars on a shirt so spectacularly awful that its very existence defies easy explanation.

Predictably lamentable drinking follows, as a large group of hostellers, including my new friend Amber, who has a tattoo of an octopus covering the entire front of her body and bright orange dreadlocks, head for an 'Irish Bar.' Or O'Irish, as my brother would call it - delineating real Irish bars from those that consider the height of Irishness to be Bud-light and shamrocks everywhere. The highlight of the evening is being introduced to a local tequila based cocktail known only as "The Mexican Muthafucker."

While you have to admire the enthusiasm of the locals getting into the StPD spirit, you do have to question the depth of their knowledge when it comes to Irish culture: yes they have put green food dye into all the lager making it taste like a swimming pool, but when one local asks me if the game on the big screen is rugby (it is, and Ireland are busy giving the Scots a good seeing to) it makes you wonder. Never mind, consolation is to be found in San Diego's worst Mexican fast food joint: what it lacks in culinary quality it makes up for in generous opening times. In my beer sodden state I order the 'giant mixed fish burrito.' The small man behind the counter takes an audible intake of breath and blows out his cheeks before disappearing into the kitchen to lovingly prepare my order.

Relieved to make it into the next day largely unscathed I take another stroll up Ocean Beach to take in one of its genuine tourist attractions: Dog Beach. Dog beach is the only area in California where dogs can run free as God intended without a lead. Unfortunately they are also free to shit as God intended which makes jogging there a perilous activity. The dog's owners take something of a laissez faire approach to cleaning up after their dogs, as I'm fairly sure God did not intend.

Back at the 'youth' hostel and I'm able to learn a little bit more of their business model. Essentially, the owner allows persons I will affectionately describe as drifters to live for free, providing they do a requisite three hours work per day. They receive no money for this, but in addition to a bunk bed, the owner does provide porridge at meal times. Which essentially makes this a Dickensian workhouse, albeit I'm fairly sure Oliver never played 'beer pong.' They also have to check out and spend a day sleeping rough every 28 days before checking back in to avoid any troublesome legal residency rights. Which is nice.

This leads to a fascinating mix of staff/residents, my absolute favourite of which is universally known as "Beer Nazi." Beer Nazi is somewhere in his early forties and works the night shift. His principle job is to ensure that the corridors are clear after 11, the porch clear by 10 and that nobody, and I mean nobody, drinks any alcohol after 9pm. Given the high number of socially functioning alcoholics mixed with college students on spring break, Beer Nazi's job is not an easy one, nor is it one he chooses to exercise with even a nod to common courtesy. However, if I had to work nights throwing backpackers out for drinking and shared a bunk bed with Tariq (see below) I'd probably be in a foul mood too.

Tariq is Beer Nazi's ever present bunk-mate. Despite this common bond, the relationship is not an easy one. Things got worse last week when Beer Nazi allegedly started a rumour that Tariq's cock was so diseased it was in danger of falling off. Tariq's 'job' at the hostel is to perform a small amount of admin work and to entertain the guests. Tariq interprets this by hitting on every female that comes within twenty yards, with, it has to be said, some success. Hence the aforementioned rumour. Tariq also turns out to be surprisingly good at rapping, and amazingly bad at football...

Ocean Beach is like swimming in new-age soup. Random conversations in coffee shops quickly turn onto the subject of chakras and crystals. In this spirit I find my way to the OB Dharma centre to join in their daily meditation class. The teacher of this group is genuine and well meaning, but the meditation is performed to rather loud new-age music. Unfortunately, on this occasion this included some rather loud didgeridoo music that sounds like a long and painful fart. Fortunately, in the dimmed candlelight, nobody can see me smirking. Or hear me farting for that matter. Thank God for incense.

Later, back at the hostel, scary mature woman reads my fortune and does some sort of astrological jiggery pokery. Turns out to be pretty accurate stuff as it goes. But it does not include sleeping with her in the immediate future. Thank God.

On the way back to the dorm, my cheeky chirpy chappie Liverpudlian room-mate Dan greets beer Nazi with the words "Alright man, just keeping it real eh?" Beer Nazi flashes a look back that silently says that there are worse things one man can do to another than kill him. Not for the first time this holiday I go to bed slightly concerned.

My training holiday is coming to an end. The final wrestling sessions are taken by a fearsome, if friendly, man called Jacko. Jacko looks like Action Man would look like if he was aged about 45, had killed slightly too many people during his action career, recently split with Barbie and developed a penchant for gin. Having detailed how to perform an extremely painful and possibly lethal spine lock submission, Jacko advises: "if he doesn't submit from this, you probably shouldn't fight this guy any more. Cos' he's one tough muthafucker."

At the conclusion to the session, I start telling Jacko that today is my last session. Before I can finish Jacko says: "yeah no problem at all buddy, I can spar with you." It's too late then to explain I was only going to ask to have a photo taken with him. It takes Jacko all of about five seconds to put me in a fearsome guillotine choke that could prompt you to ask whether the tai-chi class is still open. Still, it's all in good fun.

Later that evening, I enjoy a local blues bar with a new San Diegan friend. Unfortunately we are interrupted by a very drunk, short, fat, obnoxious man who seems hell bent on engaging me in a fist fight on the very thin grounds for offence that he respects the Queen of England more than I do. Because he is Protestant and I am not. I am not kidding. Fortunately, I am spared the degradation of fighting my new squat friend when he is summarily ejected by a very large bouncer who has clearly seen enough. I remain in the bar enjoying some quite fine blues till closing time.

Would that the rest of night went peacefully; I am woken at four in the morning by some very, very drunk Germans. After 20 minutes I was forced to cross the language divide through the universal babel fish that is the F-bomb, inserted liberally within a number of other choice words to ensure that their true meaning was conveyed. They quickly understood, which probably makes the 6.00am decision to set my 2 dollar alarm clock to go off at 6.15, wrap it in last night's wrestling boxer shorts and back heel them under one of the beds before leaving the room for the last time, a rather immature one. Good morning room-mates…adios San Diego

A picture tells a thousand words. In this case, none of the words are good.

The author, in a rare moment of hassle free skateboarding.

Part V

Navigating through Paradise

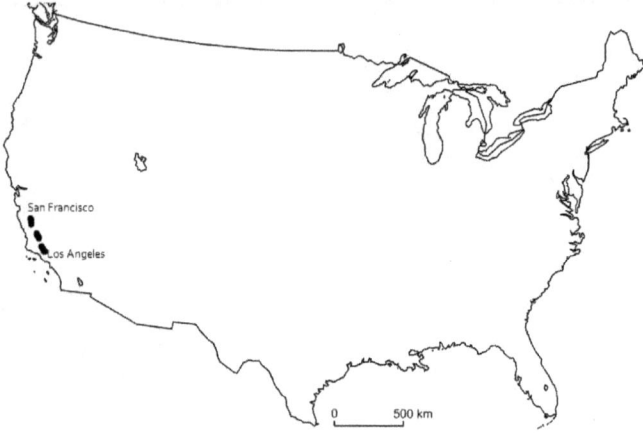

Santa Monica, LA. An undeniably nice part of town where the locals are so healthy it's disgusting. Lycra clad women strut about with yoga mats tucked under their arms, while the menfolk, seemingly with no shame whatsoever, rollerblade. I'm just so happy to be able to get a warm shower and some fresh food. After a quick trip to paddle in the Pacific, I pop into the nearest Sushi restaurant for lunch. The place is practically empty so I take a seat at the bar and get talking to the young Japanese chef. He is from Tokyo and in his fairly broken English expresses a deep respect and admiration for the music of Iron Maiden. He conveys this by doing the "Maiden, Maiden, Maiden" chant, accompanied by the requisite devil horn signs. He is suitably impressed that I have met Bruce Dickenson (HMV, York, about 14 years ago) and nods his head in approval. He poses the question: "So, you like Japanese food?" I give the affirmative and he nods again, disappearing into the kitchen. He comes back with his signature sushi dish, on the house. While I'm eating, he goes again, coming back with a lunch box packed with sushi. "Take, take, take" he insists and I leave the restaurant with enough free sushi for a top draw dinner later.

Later that evening, I'm in the hostel lounge when I hear a familiar voice "Fuck me Lee, look, its Jamie." I turn around to see none other than British John and his erstwhile travelling companion, drinking companion and all round nice guy, Lee. The last time I saw Lee and John was on Miami Beach, about 3000 miles east. By happy coincidence they have decided that Santa Monica is the place to be. This alone provides reason to celebrate, and it's onto the town with the addition of two English girls, Maddy and Sarah, and a token American, Chris. After some moderately heavy drinking I realize that, how to put this, my presence on the beach is inadvertently interfering with the amorous intent of some of our party, so I make my excuses and turn in for the night.

The next day Lee and John entertain me with stories of their travels. I come to believe that Lee and John are the Bert and Ernie of the youth hostelling world, except that Bert and Ernie never had the brainwave of mixing Jagermister with Monster Energy drink, thereby creating a brew so potent it may one day replace Crystal Meth as the drug of choice for the completely fucking insane. As travelling companions they are not best suited. Lee enjoys museums and cultural sightseeing, and has dragged a reluctant John to some of America's highlights. John does not like museums. Or reading placards, guides or if we are being honest, books. Possibly failing, therefore, to appreciate its full historical context, John sums up the visit to the Liberty Bell in Philadelphia thusly:

"Its shit."

The Grand Canyon similarly fails to impress "It's a big fucking hole; you only need to take one photo and leave. Look, here's the photo..." Worst of all however is Elis Island, historic passing point for every immigrant into America. Lee takes John on the ferry over. Imagine then,

John's horror when he realises that the whole island is one big museum, there is no bar, and the return ferry has left. And the museum itself? "Shit. Unless you enjoy reading a big list of fucking names in a big fucking book..."

During the day, I bike uptown to train at the renowned Rickson Gracie Jiu-Jitsu training centre. Its mid-day and the local news reports that it is the hottest day in LA, ever. It's so hot that the thermometer at the news station has broken. I hope the air con at the dojo is working.

Rickson Gracie is the Elvis Presley of jiu-jitsu- a man who is, by general (if not unanimous) consensus, the greatest jiu-jitsu player to have ever lived and this makes his academy something of a Mecca for BJJ tourists like me. Walking into the lobby reveals a cornucopia of memorabilia - trophies from his days fighting in Japan, and photos of fighting with the best competitors of the day. These days however Rickson is retired, and from all accounts spending increasing amounts of time in his home town of Rio, so it's no surprise not to see the man himself. The evening classes are taught by his prodigy son, Kron - a man who looks set to repeat his father's legendary dominance, if his performances at recent competitions are anything to go by. The lunch-time classes are quieter however, and ably handled by one of Rickson's brown-belt students. I'm hoping for an easy session. Unfortunately the electric is on the blink, meaning both the lights and rather more importantly the air-con, are out of commission. Two hours of training in near dark and unbelievable heat later and I'm in a pretty revolting state, and worst of all there are no showers. The fact that everybody is equally sweat sodden is not a comfort. In an unpleasant state of disrepair, I free wheel all the way down Santa Monica Blvd, making a bee-line for the ocean, were I jump straight into the cold waters before passing out on the beach in the sun. Fortunately nobody in LA has worked out how to fleece tourists for these simple pleasures so I enjoy a cheap afternoon.

That evening, the assembled Brits head out again on the town. Much merriment ensues. On the way back to the hostel we encounter a guitar playing busker, who is essentially performing to an empty street. For a modest donation the busker lets me take over on singing and guitar playing duties. Regrettably, being mostly inebriated I forget some of the words, and most of the chords. Oh well, just like Woody Guthrie, I have now busked in LA. Lee has a go next and after a group sing song to 'Sit Down' by James, we wend our way home.

Santa Monica is undeniably cool, but this is a flying visit; the following day I'm up, say my goodbyes to Lee and John and then it's off to San Francisco, my all-time favourite city in America, and probably anywhere else. Bette Noir of the Conservative right, San Francisco is an island of liberal thinking, ideals and charity. For this reason it is beloved by scores of crazies, burnt out hippies, artists, pan-handlers, pot smokers, run-aways, rubber tramps, leather tramps, the dispossessed, the disenfranchised and the downright weird. I love it. Two hours after checking into the hostel and I'm down at 10th Planet Jiu-jistu, home of BJJ world champ, Denny Prokopos.

Denny is an interesting chap. First off, he's much, much younger than most BJJ teachers- barely twenty years old. About 5' 6", 60kg yet ridiculously flexible, Denny had a physique ideally suited for a particular form of BJJ. Denny was a college student but dropped out to train full time. This dedication was not unrewarded. Denny came under the tutelage of BJJ savant, maverick and highly controversial master Eddie 'The Twister' Bravo. Eddie Bravo made a number of highly unorthodox innovations to BJJ, leading to his own system, which he named "10th Planet Jiu-jitsu" (The 10th Planet is the name of a fairly far-fetched theory that there is a 10th planet in the solar system inhabited by aliens who live in a higher state of consciousness far advanced from our own. Eddie speculated that if these aliens did jiu-jitsu, well it would probably look like his). At any rate, Eddie's system led him to defeat the legendary Royler Gracie in the world championships and by submission no less. Bolstered by this win, which many saw as vindication for Eddie's left-field theories, he went on to become a teacher of some renown, and Denny is one of his top students. Proof of this was evidenced when earlier this year, Eddie chose Denny to become his first ever black-belt, high praise indeed. This has been something of a break out year for Denny, as following his promotion he went on to win the FILA world championship (the biggest wrestling organization that is recognized by the Olympics) and placed third in the black belt division of the no gi World Championships- no small achievement at a first attempt. A lot of this, I'm sure, is down to the extraordinary self confidence that he exudes when it comes to jiu-jitsu. Shortly after being awarded his black-belt, Denny was asked by an interviewer if he ever had any doubt he would make it: "No, None at all." He sounded like he meant it. Denny likes to tell his students that he may have dropped out of college but he has a PhD in jiu-jitsu. It's a reasonable comparison - both requiring roughly the same amount of time, money, and dedication. Still, Denny rolls out this line quite a bit, but if it is indicative of any complex, such doubts would be misplaced: Denny has his own club, operating out of the fiercely anti-corporate gym: Valencia St Muscle, and is running a successful business.

Valencia St Muscle: I love this place. Some years ago, sat at University and bored of writing up my Master's thesis, I got drunk, booked a plane ticket to California and ended up in San Francisco for a month, spending my days writing in the various coffee houses, and my nights training BJJ in Valencia St. I've been back every year since and now count Denny as one of my American friends. The club only does no-gi- a faster and exhausting variant of BJJ, which in truth is something of a wrestling hybrid- too intensive to gain mass acceptance, too awesome to be totally ignored. While many orthodox students of the game, especially Brazilians, dislike the 10th Planet game, many have a road to Damascus moment when they realise its power. Often, this is in a tournament when a 10th Planet practitioner catches them in a painful submission hold set up from the seemingly benign but actually highly versatile 'rubber guard' - the ballast of the whole system. Once, in Judo, I faced a German member of the Para-Olympic team. He was blind but as the instructor led him by the arm to spar with me, he looked me straight in the eye and warned me: "He's strong." He was, and though he depended solely on touch to feel out positions, I realized quickly that he was superior to me in every department. Except one: he had never felt the rubber guard. Pulling my leg over the top of his face, setting up an extremely unorthodox strangle hold known as 'the gogoplata', my opponent had literally never felt anything like it. And not being able to see it either, had no idea how to defend. In the retelling, it might seem unsporting, but my experienced opponent understood my tactics and actually started to laugh as the strangle was sunk in; it was all highly amusing for him, but I never caught him with it again. I doubt anyone else has either.

The sparring at 10th Planet is hard: Denny's students train solidly, are skilled, determined and fit. After 90 minutes I am absolutely spent and have been handed several good beatings. These are made worse as Denny likes to mess with me; breaking his close attention on the techniques being employed to roll out his terrible mock-English accent: possibly the least convincing since Dick Van Dyke wooed Mary Poppins. Under the friendly, but uncompromising pressure of the sparring, I find myself tapping the matt (the universally accepted signal of submission) with depressing regularity. Unfortunately there are no short cuts to solving this, no quick fixes or tricks. The only thing to be done is head back the next day and go through it all again. And hope that a new kid shows up...

On my way back, in order to rehydrate, I head into my favourite bar: the gloriously named, "Black Magic Voodoo Lounge;" a New Orleans inspired gothic establishment.

It's really difficult to do justice to the utter lunacy that is the Black Magic Voodoo Lounge. I'm pretty sure that if the patrons of the BMVL were sat in a regular sports bar, they would be curiosities at best, annoying weird drunks at worse. However, context is everything, and within the BMVL the utter bizarreness of the patrons is given a credibility that possibly it ought not to have. For example: Al. As far as I can tell, Al is a retired engineer who, in a long career, has most recently been responsible for designing the armour plating that protects NATO troops from IED's. This does not, however, do Al justice. Al wears pitch black Ray Ban Aviator shades, indoors, all the time. He is known to the locals as 'Pirate Al' due to said Ray-bans. Before I've even plucked up the courage to ask Al why he is wearing sunglasses indoors, he has divulged that he has been shot twice (both times in Vietnam) and stabbed twice (history gets a little shady here, but appears to be domestic related)and shows me a key chain that states '49 Certified.' Al asks me if I know what that means. I don't. He doesn't explain. Later on Liz does though, and it transpires that Al is 'protected' by the local chapter of a biker gang so fearsome that they make the Hell's Angels look like my Mother's 'Friendship Club.' Although they do also produce key chains, which does slightly detract from the overall toughness. When I do finally ask Al about the shades he states (and this is verbatim):

"Listen man, I'm just a messenger, navigating my way through paradise. And when you're navigating through paradise, it's probably best that you wear sunglasses".

I may have drunk an obscene amount of alcohol at this point, but to me, it's the best reason for wearing sunglasses I've ever heard. I grab a napkin and write it down, so as not to forget.

Ah yes drink. It is nigh on impossible to drink responsibly in the Black Magic. You can try, but when your new best friend two bar-stools down decides to buy you a triple shot of Jameson's for no other reason than he's drunker than you are, it's a forlorn hope at best. Catching some air outside, I strike up a conversation with 'Dante'. Dante is a some-time kick-boxer who has several amusing anecdotes about getting into fights in London, and the cultural differences between American and English bar brawls (it would seem that in America, it is still acceptable practice to offer another gentleman the opportunity to step outside the premises to discuss disagreements further and settle them as necessary. Dante has discovered that such Marquis of Queensbury practices when employed in the UK, are more likely to initiate a damn good-kicking from the antagonist and his gang of drunken mates).

I step back inside to be handed an almighty glass of whiskey by Dante. "Here man, I want you to try an American Whisky. Shoot it, don't sip it..."

At the head of all this chaos is Liz, the bar-keep extraordinaire. I met Liz last year and am pleased to see that she is still here, albeit she is now basically running the place, and running it with a rod of steel. She expertly keeps all the drunken bar-flies, tourists, business men and regulars in line, while simultaneously plying them with copious quantities of booze. This is an impressive balancing act: imagine your head-teacher telling off a class of unruly children while simultaneously serving vodka-cranberry to them, and you get the idea. Earlier on in the evening Liz moves me to a different end of the bar: I had been sitting next to a harmless, but fairly annoying drunk, who kept forgetting my name. Liz explains that she is shortly going to be bouncing him out, and it appears that my 'niceness' is just going to get in the way. Best I'm at the other end, out of harm's way.

The drinking goes on for several hours with a party like atmosphere developing. Karl, on the barstool next to me, is the spitting image of Lemmy from Motorhead, including the cowboy hat and double skull rings. Karl explains that he is an events manager for a local computer games firm: "If the games company was a rockband, I'd be the road manger..." At the end of the night Karl gives me a massive bear hug and implores me: "Keep true to your ideals man, whatever you do stick by them" before stumbling out into the night. Not that I'm in any position to moralise on sobriety: Liz makes me walk around the bar so that I can appreciate just how much booze she has put into the last two Long Island Ice Teas. We collectively decide that I should probably switch to something a little easier. By 2.30am I'm done, and, having reached the considered conclusion that the Black Magic Voodoo Lounge is the greatest bar in America, stagger off to the hostel, where I sleep deeply.

Until 8.am that is, when I am woken by my one and only room-mate with the shouted words "GOOD MORNING! ITS 8AM YOU KNOW!" I can't work out if my roomie is bi-polar or simply very annoying, but practically speaking it makes no difference at this stage as he immediately wishes to discuss guns and the state of America. Through my bloodshot bleary eyed vision I can make out a 40 something American Male. He appears to be talking about Glocks. I explain my position that while the Glock 17 has a smooth and rapid rate of fire, I prefer something with a bit more stopping power, like the Ruger 38. special. He seems more than satisfied with this response, and wishing me a good morning again, he collects his rucksack and leaves. I never see him again.

This time yesterday, I was woken in similar circumstances by a Japanese gentleman who, having seen my judo-gi hanging up, wished to discuss combat and the martial arts. There are some conversations that really would be better if you weren't hung-over, half asleep/dead and, save for a sheet, totally naked. Sometimes I hate hostels.

I spend the day checking out the sights - first off it's down to North Beach. Not actually a beach per-se, but a little neighbourhood sandwiched between the financial district and Chinatown. These days North Beach is a total hole at night- it's all strip bars and gangs of drunken young men looking for trouble. Not so different from any town centre in the UK except that being San Francisco several of the strip bars are lesbian-worker-owned-collaboratives. Ethical lap-dancing, who knew? In the day time it's different; there is still a lively bohemian café culture that first attracted the beats in the 1950's. Ginsberg, Kerouac and Burroughs were regulars in these parts, and the 'City Lights' bookstore where they would hold poetry readings is still going strong, and open till midnight for late night musings and worthy activities. I buy a copy of 'Howl', and depart to Café Trieste to read it. Not bad actually. Next door to City Lights is the Vesuvio bar, where the beats used to hang out and get drunk when they weren't being worthy, reading poetry or taking part in free-form jazz nights. Vesuvio is actually still a great place to go for a drink, and not the overpriced tourist trap like you might expect.

North beach, and in fact, most of San Francisco also has more spaced out crazy people on street corners than any other city on Earth. Where did they all come from? They surely can't all be refugees from the summer of love, ground zero for which is just a few blocks away in the storied district of Haight Ashbury (now *there* is a tourist trap). Either way, there are many people here who really, really shouldn't have taken the brown acid.

I have a little time for some shopping so I make for the local branch of "On-the-Mat" which exclusively sells fight gear and jiu-jitsu related stuff. Best of all, they have a special offer where if you show up with a fresh cauliflower ear, you get ten percent off any purchase. Seriously. One new pair of shorts later and then back at 10th Planet where I do a little better on the mats, hitting an electric chair sub, a mounted gogoplata, darce, triangle and north south choke: yes, you have to love BJJ terminology. A quick change around then it's out on the town. Liz is giving me a tour of North Beach's finest drinking establishments before we head back to the BMVL. Turns out that the brewery of Rogue Dead Guy Ale is based on North Beach and has its own bar. We step inside to find that the staff are inexplicably dressed in medical scrubs. The bartender serving me has a name badge that reveals his title to be "DR Awesome". Transpires it is a charity night: 'Pints for Prostates,' where all proceeds go to a local cancer charity.

The following morning I awake to discover that the magic bike has done a magic disappearing trick: left locked outside the BMVL, someone has clearly figured out that my 'diamond proof bulldog chain,' is not as impregnable as the marketing would have you believe. Oh well, it looks like I'm hoofing it on foot now, at least Woody Guthrie would have approved. That said, there aren't many folding blue mountain bikes with a 'bikes for you.com' sticker on them, and if I ever see somebody riding one, I'm punching them in the back of the head. Woody would have approved of that too.

So, lighter of possessions, I get ready to head North, to Seattle. Anyone who liked guitar music and was a teenager in the mid-90's will hold Seattle in a certain glowing affection. I hope that it's as cool as I imagine. I hope nobody steals any more of my stuff.

The author with the crew of 10th Planet Jiu-Jitsu, SF. Denny is front middle.

The Beach Front, Santa Monica

Lee, John and I. A bit dark, but then, that's how I remember it too.

Ubiquitous tram, San Francisco

Teaching Buddha, Golden Gate Park, San Francisco

Part VI

Not Really Safe. Or Legal.

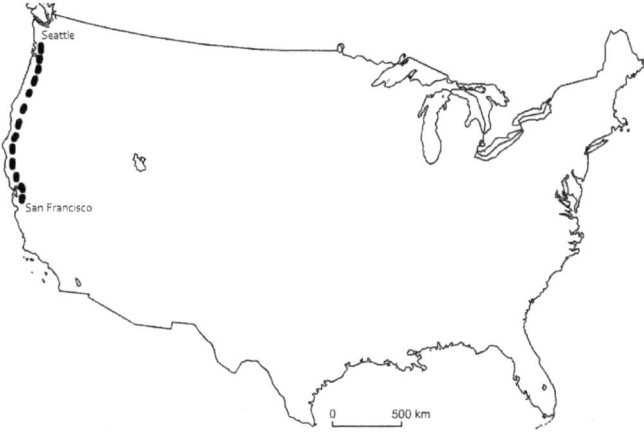

At ten o'clock at night I board a coach for Emeryville. This short trip then puts me on the overnight train all the way to the Pacific Northwest, Seattle, and my friend Amber, who I met while youth hostelling in San Diego. Amber has kindly volunteered a sofa for me to sleep on, and the promise of seeing the real Seattle. I, for my part, have promised not to produce a copy of the 'Lonely Planet' or do any lame tourist related thing that will result in her losing street credibility. I will make good on at least one of these promises....

The train is called 'The Coast Starlight,' which is a slightly more romantic a name than 'the 15.45 from Dagenham.' The route features some of the most stunning country that America has to offer, and is generally considered (probably by people who wear socks with sandals and play with model trains) to be one of the world's great rail journeys. But it's night time now, the train has been going since LA, and the assembled travellers have already slipped into 'quiet mode', including my designated 'chair buddy.' Now, the chairs on Amtrak are well equipped and of a generous size. However, they do not have any sort of divide between them, like an armrest. You also do not get a choice of who (if anyone) you will be sharing a double seat with. So, in the great Amtrak lottery, my seat buddy wins me. By the time I get there he is spread out over both seats, and clearly looking forward to an uninterrupted night of solo sleeping. He is not pleased to see me. I politely point out that I will be taking the seat next to him. "Oh. Right. I better move my stuff..." I start to get myself settled as he moves his cases. Twenty minutes later it becomes apparent that my seat buddy is not coming back. Sure enough I find him embedded and sparko in the lounge car, where he remains for the entire 24hr trip. Miserable old bastard. On the plus side, it does mean that I get an uninterrupted night of solo sleeping and a huge double seat all to myself during the day. Score. It's not even like I was going to insist on going 'big spoon.' First.

Settled in, I grab a whiskey and coke from the bar, just to take the edge off, put 'Nirvana Unplugged' on the headphones, and drift off.

Morning. Oregon. I'm woken at about 8am by an announcement that the lounge car is open for breakfast. A bit woozy, I make my way across and am seated at a table with four 'Seniors', as they call them here. Amtrak is a funny thing. Anybody with any money/sense travels the US by air. Anyone with neither of those things travels by Greyhound bus. Amtrak sits in the middle; almost as expensive as flying, almost as slow as the Greyhound. This means that the only people who want to travel by Amtrak have their own reasons for doing so: maybe for the sights, the people or the experience. My breakfast companions are just such folk, heading from LA to Portland to see the country. Barbara is about 70 and very outspoken. She is amazed/aghast that I have a girlfriend understanding enough to let me go off by myself for a month. She then recalls that after she married for the first time, her husband used to travel for months at a time on business: "It was ok. I mean, you learn to do all sorts of things by yourself when you are alone..." I catch the faintest hint of a wry smile on Barbara's face and realize that I am being flirted with by a 70 year old woman. Outstanding.

Barbara's travelling companion, sat next to me, is mercifully more restrained. Her name is Liz and she tells me that she has four sons. Liz wants to know what I do for a living, and after telling her, she goes on to tell the story of how her youngest nephew joined the New York Fire Department, of how he was one of the first to the scene on 9/11, and of how they never found him when the first tower came down. I tell Liz of how my work and the local Fire Brigade hold joint commemorative parades outside a dedicated plaque in front of the Fire Station. Her eyes well up some and she smiles and says "Thank you." Nobody talks for a bit and focus instead on the coffee and juice.

After amusing my breakfast companions with stories of the Royal family for about twenty minutes (my Prince Philip impersonation going down especially well, at last) the mood is lightened and, wishing them a good journey, I make my way back to my seat.

Mid-morning, and after a few more pages of WG's book, I head for the cafe with my chess set, where I set about playing my frustratingly good phone. Several tables over, two heavy set, deep sea crab fishermen are chatting up a girl and attempting to buy her whiskey. She spies me and jumps up saying: "Chess, cool, can I play?" before sitting herself down. The fishermen are noticeably non-plussed by this development and are giving me the hard once-over. Eventually, one comes and sits at the next table. I try to focus on the four knights defence that my new opponent, Sarah, is rolling out. "Where you from then?" enquires the larger of the two fishermen. "London" I tell him, suspecting that he is not overly familiar with Cherry Hinton. Nor do I want him to be. "Hmmmm. You like to box - Marquis of Queensbury right?" This is not really want you want to hear from a 17 stone fisherman who is perplexed at his sudden lack of female attention. "Nope. Not anymore. Now I just do Jiu-jitsu, Judo, MMA and a little bit of wrestling." This throws the Fisherman off his step for a moment. I would normally shrink from such a ridiculous display of bravado but I sense that he's looking for an opening, and I would much rather put him off kilter. "Hmmmm. I saw me some of that on TV once." He gets up and goes back to his seat. I finish my game with a less than artful checkmate, and am relieved when Sarah thanks me for the game and moves on.

On safer ground at the bar I chat to Aaron, the extrovert Amtrak barman extraordinaire. Aaron makes many, entirely unwarranted announcements over the trains PA system, providing regular updates on the state of the cafe and the temperature of the Red Bulls. Aaron would be better suited to the role of radio DJ, but for now he's doing this, and loving it. "Ladies and Gentlemen-welcome to the Coast Staaaaarlightttttttt-ahhhh. We have many cold, cold red-bulls, amongst other drinks and sundries..." Aaron enquires as to my line of work, and then greats me warmly as 'Sarge' every time I pop downstairs for a Pepsi and snacks. Behind the till he has drawn his own wanted poster in biro of a man he claims stole skittles.

By late afternoon we are passing through some of the most beautiful country I've ever seen, in America or elsewhere. Endless giant pine-tree forests and tree lined mountains under a cloudless sky. We role out of Oregon and into Washington State, where the land changes to rolling fields and streams: farm country. As we pass into Washington, Aaron makes an announcement:

"Ladies and Gentlemen, we are now entering Washington State, where it is illegal (long pause)... to hide ice cream in your pockets, pretend to have rich parents, or paint polka dots on the flag. We will not be enforcing these rules, but please, no smoking on board. If you are caught smoking on board, you will be removed from the train and taken to a secret Eastern European prison. Thank you." The carriage is a mixture of chuckles and confused looks. I pop down to see Aaron: "Ok Aaron, that last one clinched it: you're going in my blog". "Alright" he shouts back, giving me a hi-five: "I made it into the blog!"

The late afternoon sun lights up Mount St Helens. We are far North in the country now, and I avoid any further interactions with sailors and the like in favour of a nap and some light reading. Aaron is taking a break too:

"Ladies and Gentlemen: please be aware that the Cafe Car will close in exactly six and half minutes for a scheduled employee mediation break. Namaste."

By 8pm we have arrived into Seattle a few minutes early. I take the chance to freshen up a bit then wander outside into the cool air. Its dark already and colder than California, but after the Southern heat, this is a refreshing change. I take to looking at the impressive downtown skyline, when Amber and her boyfriend Greg pull up, and are a sight for sore eyes. Truth be known I'm feeling pretty exhausted, but there is no time to waste; if I crash in this state I could be out for a whole weekend. So we head straight to the Capital Hill district, or what Amber calls 'The Gay-bourhood', and into an underground bar called 'The Cha-Cha'. The bar is only lit by red lights and this, along with the decor and decidedly alternative customers give an overall psychedelic feeling. This is only enhanced by several pints of cold beer. I am the decidedly odd one out at the table, where amongst Greg, Amber and their friends, the alternative is the mainstream. Massive and impressive tattooing, hair dying and body modification are the order of the day. Greg, for example, has the words "Laid. Back" tattooed across his knuckles. Still, everyone is very friendly and chatty over the loud rock soundtrack to the bar. No less friendly, although a great deal more scary, are the other girls we are sharing a table with. Dressed in industrial/fetish/neo-punk outfits, they make for a fearsome sight. One of the girls has the letters "FAG" tattooed across her knuckles. This strikes me as unusually aggressive, so I enquire as to her motivation for obtaining such a tat. Her friend, who with her thick black hair and femme-fatale make-up looks like Tura Satana, answers for her: "It's because she's a fucking bad-ass dyke." Oh. That answers that then. The girl just smiles demurely and nods. I'm relieved when they leave and I can have a slightly more reasonable discussion with Greg about the current state of the Seattle Seahawks.

The following day, Amber and Greg take me to the Pike Place Market, a popular tourist spot. I break my no-lame-tourist photo rule, by insisting on visiting the first ever Starbucks and posing for photos. Sad as I am to admit it, this is something of a pilgrimage to me, spending as I do, an inordinate amount of time sloping around in Starbucks. I have also read the Starbucks CEO book- the wonderfully titled "Pour your heart into it", a book with so little irony and sense of perspective (it is after all, only coffee) it's almost sinister. Some people chide me for my predilection for Starbucks with well-worn objections- so yes, it is corporate coffee, and yes it is cultural imperialism, and no the coffee isn't really all that great. However, and it's a big 'however', I've been an espresso junkie (16 shots a day at my lowest point) for many, many years and I remember what it was like in the UK before Starbucks invaded- you couldn't get a decent shot of espresso outside of London for love nor money. Café's still sold instant coffee for 40p a cup and it was acceptable for restaurants to have all-in-one fake cappuccino machines serving warm brown spew. Once, I saw a five grand Gaggia being used as a kettle to make cups of 'Maxwell House'. Starbucks changed all that. My old boss, when I used to run a café, told me that Starbucks was the greatest thing that ever happened to him because it convinced everybody it was perfectly acceptable to pay two pounds fifty for warm milk. So in recognition of the former, if not the latter, I find the Pike-Place Starbucks. Of course being a chain, it looks exactly like every other bloody Starbucks anywhere on the planet. I suppose that's fitting.

Slightly more impressive is the market's cheese shop, where they sell cartons of macaroni cheese made with cheddar aged for 18months. It is fantastic. Something my strangely cheese-obsessed brother would approve of. We then head to the 'Seattle Centre', where I once again get lame photos of the iconic, but ironically pointless 'Space-needle'.

Later afternoon and, along with Ambers friends Daniel and Bree, we head to see "The Social Network," then it's back to Amber's for a fire-pit drinking session and BBQ. We are travelling now in Ambers extremely worn, if reliable, Suzuki Side-Kick. Duct tape holds my window up, and a piece of wood keeps it in place. Grass is growing in the carpet and out of the door. "Now I have to warn you," Says Amber "that this car isn't exactly safe. Or legal."

Against the odds, we arrive back home, equipped with wine and fire-wood. We sit out at Amber's fire-pit for a few hours, drinking and talking. I attempt to impress by making my signature dish of hot potato crisps (slice thin, butter, salt pepper, flat wrap in tin foil, throw on flames) which goes down well. Seattle defies its reputation by not raining, and we stay up late till the rose wine is gone, leaving only a warm fuzzy feeling in my head.

In the morning my flying visit to Seattle has almost come to an end. I have a relaxing morning catching up on my laundry and chatting over coffee with Amber and her friend Bree, who both work in the wonderfully titled: "Slave to the Needle," where Greg is a resident tattooist. It transpires that the shop also does body piercing. Amber and Bree explain, in detail that frankly I'd rather forget, the ins and outs (which is an unfortunate turn of phrase under the circumstances) of genital piercing. Decency prevents me from going into any more detail, suffice to say that if anybody ever suggests that you go for 'pearling,' politely decline. And leave town.

Endless forests, somewhere in Oregon

Amber and Greg

Not really safe, or legal

On board chess: More dangerous that it looks

Part VII

Just a Knife

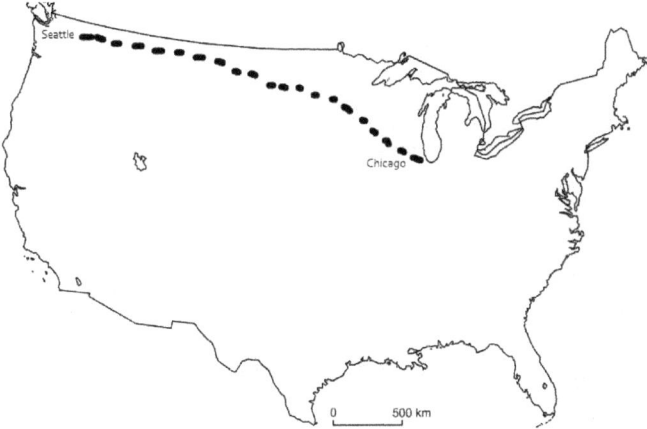

Amber drops me off at the station and I catch the afternoon train from Seattle to Chicago with minutes to spare. The train is another gigantic 'Superliner' with the justifiably grandiose title "The Empire Builder." This is the train route that opened up the West for the better, and for a great many, the worse.

The coach class is thinly populated; the majority of people prepared to take 48 hours to travel to Chicago are also prepared to shell out extra for a room with a bed. This means that the occupants of the couple of economy coaches who don't have suites are virtually all young, poor and funky looking, and creates a bit of a hostel atmosphere. This suits me just fine, and I settle down to watch the Washington scenery go by. I'm feeling strangely deflated, maybe because I'm heading back East, or maybe it's the cloud covered countryside. This is, after all, the North West territory which, a certain currently popular teen fiction author would have you believe, turns all adolescents into sulky, pining, whiny emos. Or big fucking werewolves.

After a couple of hours it's dark and I head up to the deserted dining car. Eventually I'm joined by Emily, a young woman who has just completed walking the Pacific Trail- 2700 miles of dirt trails and mountain tracks-puts my own little journey into perspective, that's for damn sure. Emily has been doing this alone, meeting people on the way, which is pretty impressive stuff, although she also works in construction, suggesting that she is far from being a shrinking violent. We talk for a while about bears. There are many established strategies for dealing with a bear encounter. There are also many dead hikers who would testify to their general inefficacy, if only they were able. The surest, and by far the easiest, is to simply buy a gun. But this simplicity is deceptive. Black bears are generally the least confrontational and will likely run from a warning shot. But Grizzlies are another matter entirely. Anything less than a magnum round from a handgun is unlikely to be more than a general inconvenience to a Grizzly. Rifles offer more chance, but then there is the matter of aiming and firing. Anyone who can hold their nerve and get off a kill shot at short range to a charging grizzly is made of stern stuff indeed. Emily didn't carry a gun. She opted instead for 'bear mace' a mini-fire extinguisher size can of pepper spray. I'm impressed, but frankly uncertain as to the wisdom of this. Sure it removes the need for the steel-like nerves necessary to get off a single shot, but on the other hand if it doesn't work, that's going to be one angry, angry bear. I decide that if I ever walk the Pacific trail, I'm taking nothing smaller than an Uzi. Same goes for walking in Detroit, but that's another story. I turn in for the night, enjoying the peace of a near empty carriage and hoping that I don't dream of bears. Or Detroit.

Morning. We're out of Washington State now and somewhere in Montana. Overnight we passed briefly through Idaho, and are now deep into the 'Big Sky' state. Just before 8am we stop for our first break of the day, in a small rural town called Shelby. I step outside into the cold morning air. A chill wind blows through the station. I've managed to extend my summer into early October by staying in the Southern States, but this is the far North and its definitely Fall here. The smokers are unusually quiet, and pace up and down the platform keeping warm. I stroll down the far end of the station and take a look at the town. A huge painted sign advertises 'Lumber' but nothing else leaps out. The town seems to end where the last resident pitched his trailer. The look of the passengers boarding here is different to Seattle. Boots, baseball caps and lumberjack shirts are de-rigeur and the people look as hard-bitten as the place itself. I chat for a couple of minutes with one such traveller, whose itinerary seems to have gone awry: "Dang! I'm stuck in Shelby for two days! Dang…" Suddenly I realize that the train has boarded and is getting ready to pull away. Not wishing to be stuck with him for the next two days, I apologise and sprint for the doors, while making a mental note to use the word 'Dang' more often in conversation.

Back on board and it's off to the dining car for breakfast. My breakfast companions this morning are Wes and his wife Liz. Wes is retired and has the steely look and 'high and tight' hair cut that suggests service with the Marine Corp. Wes is polite but guarded and seems a bit suspicious of me so we keep the talk light, discussing the recent concussion of the Chicago Bears quarterback and their subsequent prospects for the season (mixed, in case you were wondering). Slowly Wes warms up, he doesn't like my work too much but likes my various Royal Family stories, and reveals that he served in the Marines in the 50's. I score more points by knowing that his base - Camp Pendleton, is the home of the legendary 'Heartbreak Ridge,' and after telling some of my brother's stories about interactions with the American military he loudly proclaims "Ha! I like you" banging his hand on the table for emphasis.

The day passes slowly, but not disagreeably. The mountains of Montana even out into the endless rolling grasslands of horses, cattle and white picket fences. Everybody seems relaxed in each other's company, including the train staff, who will be with us for the whole journey from Seattle to Chicago. In the evening, Emily and I meet up for a game of chess. Earlier on at lunchtime I noted that Emily was cutting herself pieces of cheese to eat with a serrated edge hunting knife. "That's one heck of I knife" I remarked. "Nope" she replied turning it over and considering it for a moment, "It's just a knife."

At any rate, Emily transpires to be ludicrously competitive, maybe too competitive for a girl who also happens to be packing bear-mace. "Bitch!" she loudly exclaims as I execute a Queen/Rook forked check that will shortly end the game.

The sun sets slowly over the Montana grasslands, and deciding against trying to get my beer-on with Amtrak prices, I take an early night.

Morning. Finally out of Montana, we've spent much of the night passing through the mostly empty state that is North Dakota. Of course, the pioneers took it off the resident Indians anyway. These Northern barren states were once the home to many Indian Nations and the train rolls through some historic sights. We pass Fort Buford where Chief Sitting Bull surrendered, but not before he and Crazy Horse gave Custer's troops a well-deserved spanking at the battle of the Little Big Horn. Also visible from the train are the Bear's Paw Mountains, where in 1877 Chief Joseph, of the Nez Perce Indians, finally surrendered to the US Army after an astonishing 1700 miles in retreat, still one of the greatest in all military history, marking the end of the Indian wars and the start of their slow demise on reservations. Upon surrendering, Chief Joseph, clearly a man who knew a thing or two about sound-bites, said: "Hear me, my chiefs, I am tired. My heart is sick and sad. From where the sun now stands, I will fight no more forever." He kept true to that promise, although his ancestors would eventually take a terrible revenge in the form of reservation casinos and video poker.

By breakfast time we have arrived into Minnesota, and the large station serving the twin cities of Minneapolis and St Paul. At the smoke break in Minneapolis I slip un-noticed into the first class lounge next to the platform and score myself some complimentary coffee. It's the end of the pot, has been stewing for God knows how long, and only fills half the cup, but it's strong, hot and the caffeine gives me a buzz enhanced by the mild naughtiness of its origin. Better still, Minneapolis has a choice of newspapers and I score a copy of the New York Times for the first time in days. Heading back East, back to the world of big, important looking newspapers.

At breakfast, I meet my first celebrity of the trip, although I am fairly sure that she would blanch at such a description. Learning that I am writing a book she would rather not be named, so let's just give her a randomly assigned initial of 'R'. R is an author, who writes gothic tinged suspense thrillers of an emo bent aimed at a young adult audience. She is travelling West from giving the keynote address at a writers conference and savours the break that travelling by train affords. We chat for about three hours and I pick up many insider truths about the publishing industry - like the fact that authors get little choice in their book covers, or sometimes the titles. Including the word 'Hell' in the title will lead to its exclusion from many school reading lists, and it's advisable not to use the f-bomb in the text, that is if you want to get it into school libraries. R also advises me that the big bucks are to be made in writing about vampires. Good to know.

Later that day, I meet a beautiful but emotionally troubled and angst ridden vampire, and embark on a number of romantic adventures. The end.

By late afternoon the familiar Chicago skyline appears on the horizon. I'm relieved, and looking forward to a meal, a pint and a hot shower. I give Emily a goodbye hug and agree to meet up for online chess soon. Out of the station, it's surprisingly warm. Happy to walk under the blue-sky later afternoon sun, I make for my hostel in the leafy and lovely Jackson Park district. I was here a year ago and I have some happy memories staying at this hostel. 'The Getaway' is ridiculously opulent and about as far from the traditional ratty/paternal youth hostel as you can get. Leather sofas and plasma screen tv's, marble floors and high speed wi-fi. Guitars are available to borrow, and bikes to rent. When I visit the staff are organizing a wine-tasting and are quick to offer me a glass. Nice touch, but after 48 hours on a train it's not what I need right now. I aim for a quick turn-around: Showered and changed I go right back out again to find the aforementioned pint. Jackson Park is populated by predominately white affluent Chicagoans and walking about is like being warped into an Abercrombie and Fitch catalogue. Still, I'm glad to be back in Chicago, the town has a buzz and a vibe that is difficult to describe. Hence the need to use the revolting terms 'vibe' and 'buzz'. Sat in a friendly bar entitled "The Other Side" I sup on some domestic brew and read the local paper -President Obama has been back in town today, trying desperately (and it transpires fruitlessly) to save his former Senate seat from falling into Republican hands. Maybe if he'd done a couple of public rallies for the people who voted for him rather than a fundraising dinner for the extraordinarily rich he might have had more luck. The beer quickly works its magic and I find that I'm beat from travelling and turn in for an early night in a real bed. Even if it is a real bunk bed with a sweating, farting and regrettably masturbating Armenian gentleman ensconced immediately below me.

Rising early I check my email. To my horror I have been sent a race day reminder by the New York Runners Association that I foolishly signed up to before coming to America. At the time, I was looking for a literal finish line for my long journey, and when I saw that they were holding the NYC Staten Island Half Marathon the day before I flew back, it seemed just perfect. But my debit card didn't seem to process, I heard nothing, and largely forgot about the matter. My debit card did process, and they are now happily expecting my attendance on Sunday morning, in three days' time. I'm not sure that my beach volleyball and 1 mile run with my God Daughter in Houston is adequate preparation for distance running. In a slight panic, I head out for a run to test my conditioning. I do a steady 7.5 miles at a moderate pace along the shore of Lake Michigan. Not bad, and enough to hope that maybe Sunday's race won't be a complete disaster. I set a target time of finishing. That'll be just fine for this year.

Before leaving the hostel I give myself a haircut with the $10 clippers I bought in Miami. Misreading the grade of the plastic attachment I proceed to near scalp myself, and with my ever growing beard now look like a bonafide maniac. Super. I would have been better off waiting for

Eduardo. At least it gives me an excuse to buy a Chicago Bears baseball cap. 'How bout dem' Bears' etc, etc.

At 9.30pm I board the night train for New York City. The end of my round America trip is a tantalisingly short 23 hours, and a few hundred miles away. If I can just avoid lunatic fishermen, knife wielding outdoorsy types who don't like losing and under-estimating the time it takes to retrieve a copy of The Times from a station building during a cigarette break, I'll be just fine.

Mountain Railroad, Washington State

Twin flags, Downtown Chicago

Part VIII

The Finish Line

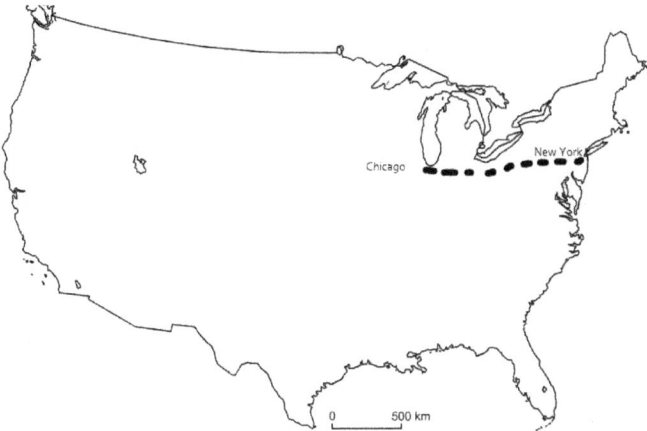

The train from Chicago to New York leaves at nine thirty at night. Waiting in line to check baggage, a short Chinese woman literally barges me out of the way with a muttered 'excuse me' and goes to the desk. I'm within ear shot when the Amtrak attendant explains to her that her ticket is for tomorrow, not today, and that she has 24 hours to wait. Wow. Instant karma really is going to get you.

Having waited patiently in line, I discover that I have no similar ticketing issues and safely board the train. Unlike my previous journeys, this is a popular route, and every seat is sold. The carriages are packed, and the crowd is decidedly different; less travellers and day-dreamers, and more commuters. The staff seem more harassed and the atmosphere less relaxed. Fortunately, I have bought with me my own quarter bottle of relaxation and stroll to the lounge car to order a glass of Pepsi, which I then infuse with a hefty glug of Jack Daniels, technically in breach of Amtrak's alcohol policy. Sitting opposite me is Sandrine- a French woman who is nursing a glass of wine. She smiles broadly "Ah yes, yes, yes - for a more relaxed journey, non?" Yes indeed. Having established a clear understanding Sandrine and I chat for a while. I certainly would not ask her age, but at a rough guess I'd say 55. Hard to tell because Sandrine wears a lot and I do mean a lot, of makeup. Transpires she is a professional make-up artist, originally from Paris, now living and working in New York. She loves it but still can't find a decent bottle of vino: "These Californian wines…. I mean, some of them are not too bad but…" I ask Sandrine if she has any famous clients - she does, but is far too discrete to name names. She is more keen to discuss my love life. I show her a photo of my girlfriend: "Ah yes yes, very pretty, very pretty. Does she wear much makeup?" I explain that my girlfriend never leaves the house without her make up. "Ahhh, yes, yes, good girl!" Clearly the right answer then. Further elaborations on my girlfriend's beauty routine, which for reasons of discretion I will leave out, elicit similar positive responses, and I am cautioned, in the strongest terms, never to be critical of the time invested in such rituals. Duly chastened I bid Sandrine good night and head back to my chair, where, despite the presence of a young family to the left and right of me, I manage to sleep for the next eight hours.

The night's sleep ends abruptly when at about 8am I am gently but firmly woken by a US Immigrations Official.

"Sir, Sir- Are you a US citizen?"

"Wha-eh-ah-who- what?"

"Are you a US citizen?"

"Oh, right. No."

This answer leads to a thorough inspection of my passport, after which I am free to go and get coffee. Strangely, everybody who simply answered 'yes' to that question was left alone. Hmmm. I'm not an expert, but I find some loop holes in that investigation strategy.

At any rate, my brush with the authorities over, the train continues to make its way and I go to the dining cart, where I take a short mid-morning nap. This comes to an abrupt end when I am woken by a train guard:

"Sir- are you going to Boston?"

"Wha-eh-who- what?"

"Are you going to Boston Sir- if not you need to get back to your seat- this dining car is going to Boston."

Not realising that the dining car had made alternative plans for the day, I reclaim my seat. I'm now sitting next to a young man from the family surrounding my seat, who has clearly decided that I'm not all that scary after all, and has switched seats with his mother to sit next to me. I notice after a few minutes that he has started to imitate my English accent, much to the amusement of his younger sister. Playing along I teach him a number of key English phrases. He disappears off to the restroom remarking loudly that the train's current delay "Is just not cricket…"

By mid-afternoon we are following the Hudson river into New York. The countryside of New York State is very pretty in the Fall, with the leaves beginning to go a range of yellows and browns. This is less album cover America, and more biscuit tin box America. By six-thirty the Manhattan sky line looms into view and we pull into the sprawling Penn Station where I started my journey, nearly a month previously. Leaving the train, I climb the stairs and stand in the station concourse. I get a feeling of achievement- I've done roughly 8000 miles in this round trip, most of it rooted firmly to the ground. This sense of achievement is muted by the knowledge that it doesn't take a great deal of skill to read a route map, or physical exertion to sit on your arse while travelling at 70mph. However, achievement nevertheless and certainly enough to warrant the purchase of a celebratory six pack of domestic brewed beer which I take with me to the hostel.

This time I'm staying at my all-time favourite youth hostel- "The Wanderers Inn, West." It's my favourite, purely because it is the first one I ever stayed in, for nearly a month, and I therefore hold it in an affection that is out of synch with its virtues. The ubiquitous 'Hostel World' rates it a lowly 68%, depending on who has rated it most recently. I think that it's better than that, but I can sort of see their point - the facilities are very basic; a small kitchen/common room, laundry room, and save for a pretty grubby back yard, that's it. But it is clean, it is cheap, and being so small it is very good for meeting fellow travellers, much more so than some of the mega hostels. The staff aren't pretending to be cooler than you either, which is quite refreshing for a youth hostel these days. The air-con is a bit hit and miss; on a previous visit my room became so unbearably humid in the August heat (augmented by several farting Australians) that at about 1am I had enough and, picking up my blanket, I left the hostel and made the one block walk to Central Park, where I climbed a small hill and slept under a tree until the dawn and a curious squirrel woke me up. I thought nothing of it at the time, but retelling the tale some years later to a New Yorker, he declared me "officially the most bad-ass guy I know." Apparently I was lucky not to be found and eaten by the people who live in the park. Or by Freddie the dog, I suppose.

Saturday morning and I take a relaxed stroll around the neighbourhood, heading back up to 112th and Broadway to Tom's restaurant for pancakes. I'm going to miss pancakes. Anyway, perusing the New York Times I find an unintentionally hilarious article in the 'International' section concerning the growth and liberal attitude towards public sex in Great Britain. The NY Times reports that this is a pastime that has widespread acceptance and is growing in popularity. The NY Times is a very widely read paper throughout the US, and is popular with politicos, the upper middle class and culture vultures. All of whom now have the bizarre impression that Britain is a nation of people who think nothing of going 'dogging' (they explained the origins of the word). Bizarre.

On a less light note, the Mayor of New York is proposing legislation that would prevent people using food-stamps to purchase sugary drinks. Ah, food stamps, society's way of saying 'we're comfortable with you being poor, but we don't want you to starve.' Stepping out of the restaurant, a homeless man asks me for a quarter. Given that such luxuries as Pepsi and Coke will soon be out of his reach, it seems churlish not to. At the bottom of the street, another homeless man asks me for change. On explaining that I have literally just given me change away he says "And God bless you for that" at which point he tries to give me some of HIS spare change. My baseball cap prompts a quick conversation about the continuing travails of the Chicago Bears and then the homeless man wanders off. New York is a city that can surprise you, if you let it.

I spend the rest of the day in quiet preparation/dread for Sunday's race. Although my pre-race preparations do include a couple of cheeky afternoon pints, strictly to take the edge off.

Sunday Morning. Race day. I'm not feeling confident. I couldn't find any pasta last night so my pre-race meal consisted of a Chinese take out from an extremely grubby 'restaurant.' I have to get up at 5.30am to make the journey to the other end of Manhattan in order to catch the 7.30am Staten Island Ferry. Miss this, and there is literally no way to make it to the race. At 59th St station it becomes very apparent that my connecting train is not coming anytime soon. I spot two other nervous looking people in running gear, and, after calling an impromptu conference we quickly decide to split a cab fare downtown. En-route Neke (probably spelling that wrong) and Fabrize (ditto) tell me about the course. I am relieved to learn that it is fast and flat, except for one hill right at the end. Less reassuring are their projected finish times, which are streaks ahead of mine. My stomach really feels bad now....

Runners pack the 7.30am ferry. Everybody is amiable, if nervous looking. They all have shinier running gear than me. I bet they all had pasta last night too. Still, it's a bright, sunny Sunday morning and not a cloud in the sky. On the ten minute ride to the island I remind myself of the advice that my brother gave me some time ago when I expressed trepidation at my first half marathon. He informed me that any fit adult should be capable of running a half marathon, without preparation, if they follow a simple two step plan:

Step 1: Dig in.

Step 2: Hump it.

Unfortunately, after a month's travelling and next to zero prep, this is actually the best plan that I have. Hard to believe that Runners World have never published an article on it. As we disembark, a man with a megaphone shouts directions to the runners, rounding off with "Smile folks - it's going to be a great day". We'll see.

With 5000 runners assembled on the start line, the American anthem is sung, which is nice, and then we're off. My key to distance running is to find a pace setter to follow - somebody that looks like they are running roughly the speed you want to go, just a little bit faster. My preference is for pacers who are both tall and broad, as they act as first rate wind-breakers. Having found a suitable subject, I follow him for the first three miles. My nerves are now settled, and I feel good. I ditch the pacer, speed-up and dig in. By the ten mile mark I'm both surprised and pleased to find that my pace is good, and I'm on track for a respectable time. I'm tired though. Clearly it is time to move to step two in the plan: Hump it. Fortunately, this coincides with the Rocky theme coming on my ipod. Excellent. I step up a gear for the last three miles, amused to see that a girl is clearly using me as a windbreak. Oh well. In the end I put on a sprint and come in at one hour, fifty minutes and fifty one seconds. Not bad at all, and two minutes faster than my time last year in Chicago. Clearly then, jogging as a form of exercise is massively over rated and I will desist with it immediately.

Crossing the finish line I pick up my complementary Gatorade and bagel and sit at the edge of the docks, watching the boats pass the Manhattan skyline. I've travelled 8000 miles around America and the last 13 were the hardest.

Actually, that's not true at all. I just thought it would sound good (it doesn't). Really, the hardest miles were the two dozen or so, on the train between Tucson and LA when I had the shits. But frankly that doesn't have a very poetic ring to it. Hey-ho.

I spend the rest of my time in New York on a slow walkabout, seeing places I haven't been to before, and revisiting a few fond memories in places I have. Strolling about lower Manhattan, I come upon Wall Street. It's hard not to think of this street as the scene of a crime, such is the infamy that is now associated with it. From within a couple of hundred metres of where I stand, traders bought up inconceivable amounts of bad debts, accumulated from people who were incapable of understating the deals they were signing, then sold them on as good debts, and then bet against those same debts failing. They then took insurance out on that too. Unsurprising then that something went wrong somewhere along the line. I'm glad that there wasn't a great depression; WG's account suggests that the last one was somewhat light on chuckles. I'm also glad that there is still cash in the cashpoints. I stay out of politics, but I'll say this; what happened in this street took a lot of money from the pockets of people that didn't have much to begin with, then put it into the pockets of those that did and in the fallout the US national debt doubled, thirty million people worldwide lost their jobs, their homes, their savings and their prospects. The champagne bars in this district still do good business.

I wind up my time in the slightly more pleasant environs of a café on Central Park West, sipping black coffee, reading and making chit-chat with students from the nearby Columbia University. I finish up WG's autobiography that I've been saving for the end of my journey. Woody spent most of his life travelling America by train, foot and thumb. Seriously injured in an accident after the War, and blacklisted due to his communist connections, Woody could no longer play guitar or sing. Succumbing to Huntington's disease he was hospitalized and finished his journey in New York, where a young Bob Dylan would visit and play to him on guitar. In truth, the railroads that Woody rode are now an oddity - a fairly expensive travel choice for those who can afford the luxury. If Woody were around today he would be riding the Greyhound buses and busking in service stations. Yet, there is a romance to riding the same rails and seeing the same countryside that he did.

So sitting in this café, on a warm and sunny Sunday afternoon, I'm able to reflect a bit - I feel like I've accomplished what I set out to do - I feel like I've really seen this country now. I've lost an ok bike, but made some friends, so I think I'm ahead on points.

I'm leaving America now, and true to Robert Louis Stevenson's advice, I'm travelling hopefully - I hope that the public sector is where I left it. I hope the present I have bought my girlfriend is suitable for a month's absence. I hope that I never again see somebody throw up in a yoga class. I… no, that'll do for now.

JS

New York City, 10/10/10

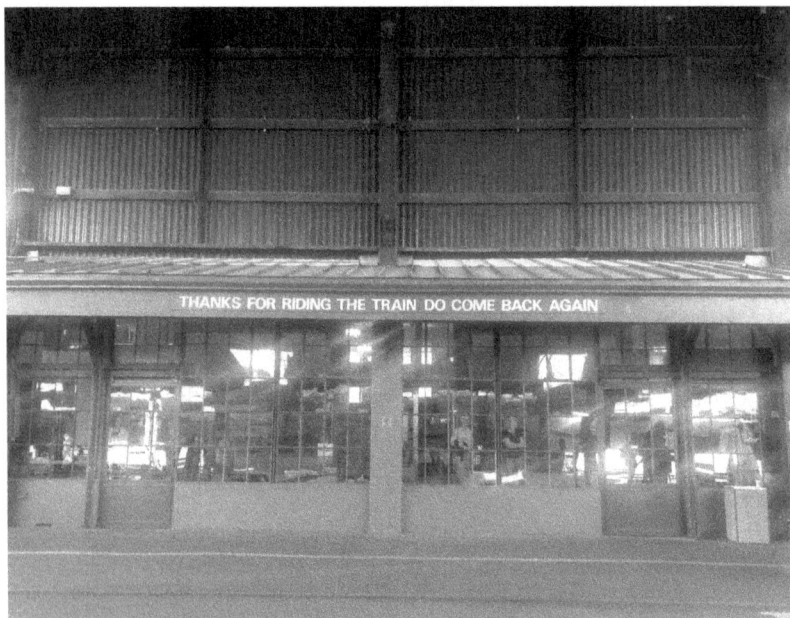

About this Book

Just like the t-shirts say, I really do love New York. In fact I love all of America. Except maybe Hank. Or Detroit. This makes it easy to romanticize some aspects of it, or not to think too deeply about others, like 'why are there so many homeless people in one of the richest cities in the world?' The hard truth is that tonight some forty thousand people, including sixteen thousand children, will be homeless in NYC. Thousands will sleep in the parks and subways and many thousands more will be dependent on soup kitchens and food banks to survive.

The primary cause for homelessness is the lack of affordable housing, coupled with a minimum wage that is far, far below the living wage. There is not much to be done about that. However, it is also true that many homeless persons suffer from drug and alcohol addiction, from mental and physical health problems and have very, very poor future prospects. This can be changed. I pledge that one hundred percent of the author's royalties from this book will be donated to a New York based charity that provides short and long term help for the homeless-helping them beat addiction, get training and education and make a meaningful and positive change in their lives. By buying this book you have helped in that. Thank you.

www.ingramcontent.com/pod-product-compliance
Lightning Source LLC
Chambersburg PA
CBHW072004060426
42446CB00042B/1821